Charles Augustus Stoddard

**Beyond the Rockies**

A Spring Journey in California

Charles Augustus Stoddard

**Beyond the Rockies**
*A Spring Journey in California*

ISBN/EAN: 9783744743808

Printed in Europe, USA, Canada, Australia, Japan

Cover: Foto ©Andreas Hilbeck / pixelio.de

More available books at **www.hansebooks.com**

AN AVENUE IN SOUTHERN CALIFORNIA

# BEYOND THE ROCKIES

## *A SPRING JOURNEY IN CALIFORNIA*

BY

CHARLES AUGUSTUS STODDARD

Editor of "The New York Observer," Author of
"Across Russia," "Spanish Cities," etc.

*ILLUSTRATED*

NEW YORK
CHARLES SCRIBNER'S SONS
1894

To
## MARY PRIME STODDARD
WHOSE COMPANY IN THIS JOURNEY
AS IN
LIFE'S LONGER PILGRIMAGE
HAS DOUBLED ITS PLEASURES AND LIGHTENED ITS CARES
THIS BOOK IS AFFECTIONATELY INSCRIBED
BY
THE AUTHOR

## CONTENTS

### I. SOUTH AND WEST

PAGE

From Winter to Spring — Plans for Mexico nipped in the Bud — A Raymond Excursion — Virginia and Tennessee — Lookout Mountain — Its Scenes and Memories ........... 1

### II. FROM THE MOUNTAINS TO THE GULF

Birmingham and its Activities — Spring in New Orleans — Beauty and Business — The Louisiana Lottery — Growth, Enterprise, and Prosperity — Dr. Palmer and his Church.. 7

### III. ALONG THE SUNSET ROAD

Louisiana and its Fertile Acres — Bayous and Rice-fields — Galveston and its Beach — Houston and its Boom — Literary Curiosities ..................................... 14

### IV. SAN ANTONIO DE BEXAR

The Border Fortress — A Thrilling History — The Alamo and its Defenders — Scenes in the Town — The Jesuit Missions — A Government Post and Evening Parade.............. 19

### V. ALONG THE RIO GRANDE

Wild and Picturesque Scenery — The Town of Langtry — A One-Man Government — Desert Views — Marathon and its Greeks — Time at El Paso............................. 24

### VI. NEW MEXICO AND ARIZONA

The Town of Juares — Over the Border — Climate and Health — Indian Villages — Sunday at Tucson — Its Schools and University ......................................... 30

## VII. ONE OF OUR INDIAN SCHOOLS

A Presbyterian Contract — Good Teachers — The Correct Idea of Indian Education — Reports from the Government Superintendent .................................................. 35

## VIII. THROUGH THE DESERT TO PARADISE

Cacti — The Colorado River — Yuma and the Indians — Below the Ocean — A California Riddle ........................ 44

## IX. IN CALIFORNIA

Climate and Weather — Varied Productions — Inhabitants — Riverside and its Oranges — Horticulture and its Results  50

## X. CORONADO BEACH

A Narrow Escape — Fine Weather — A Luxury to live — Acres of Wild Flowers — Beauty on Sea and Shore — Comfort and Good Company — Excursions — Blue Presbyterianism ................................................. 57

## XI. PASADENA

Signing Tickets — Breaking a Train in Two — Ocean Views — Meeting Dr. Ormiston — His Good Work — Friends in Pasadena — A Big Rose-Bush — The Crown of the Valley — A Model Town .......................................... 64

## XII. IN THE SAN GABRIEL VALLEY

Excursions in the Valley — Lucky Baldwin and his Ranch — Sunny Slope Vineyards — The Old Mission — A Mountain Railroad — Easter Sunday at Pasadena ................. 70

## XIII. THRIVING TOWNS

Los Angeles — A Flourishing City — Hills and Homes — Redlands and the Smileys — The Boy who wanted to be a Civil Engineer ................................................. 77

## XIV. SANTA BARBARA

Beautiful for Situation — An Earthquake — The Tale of a Patron Saint — First Impressions — A Placid Town — Natural Beauties — A Winter View ........................ 82

## XV. ROMAN CATHOLIC MISSIONS

The Padres and their Work — The Presidio and the Church — How the Missions grew — A Short, Sad History — The Lessons of the Past.... .............................. 89

## XVI. FLOWER FESTIVAL AT SANTA BARBARA

Multitudes of Flowers — Ten Thousand Roses on a Carriage — A Flower Dance — The Floral Procession — The Mayor's Proclamation ......................................... 96

## XVII. PLEASURE-DAYS AT SANTA BARBARA

The Mission Cañon — A Picnic at Ellwood — Monte Cito and its Gardens — The Hot Springs — The Ojai Valley and San Marcos Pass............................................ 104

## XVIII. ANCIENT SPANISH HOUSES

Carrillo Arguello and de la Guerra — Old Days in Santa Barbara — Feasts and Weddings — The Chinese Colony — Friends and their Work................................ 111

## XIX. HOW WE WENT TO YOSEMITE

The Crown of California Scenery — A Wily Agent — Ruts and Bogs — Fine Air and Hard Fare — An American Jolting Car — Mules and their Drivers — The Public and its Servants.................................................... 117

## XX. THE YOSEMITE VALLEY

Our Entrance — Wonderful Views — Manifold and Beautiful Waterfalls — Precipices Thousands of Feet High — Mirror Lake and Merced River — Did the Bottom drop out — Grandeur and Triviality................................. 123

## CONTENTS

### XXI. CALIFORNIA BIG TREES

Mariposa and Santa Cruz Groves — Comparisons and Measurements .................................................. 130

### XXII. HETCH-HETCHY VALLEY

An Interesting Letter — The Cañon of the Tuolumne — An Indian Hiding Place — Fish and Game ................ 137

### XXIII. EL MONTE

Rough Travelling — Monterey — Its Foundation and History — The Hotel del Monte — An Artificial Paradise — Flowers, Shrubs, and Trees — A Priest's Monument — The Old Oak — Pacific Grove — The Seventeen-Mile Drive — Seals, Shells, Buffaloes, and Bears — Strange Cypresses......... 143

### XXIV. IN THE SANTA CLARA VALLEY

Incidents at Santa Cruz — San José — Churches, Public Buildings, and Schools — Lick Observatory — Leland Stanford Junior University — Palo Alto Stables — Training School for Fast Trotters ...................................... 155

### XXV. SAN FRANCISCO

Dana's Prophecy — California Optimism — The Chinese Problem — A Curious and Composite City — Beautiful Suburbs — A Visit to Chinatown — The Theatre and Opium Dens — Chinese Men, Women, and Children — Sausalito, Ross Valley, and San Rafael — A Sudden Squall — The Presbyterian Seminary — Friends and Festivities — Sacramento.. 172

### XXVI. ACROSS THE SIERRA TO SALT LAKE

Sacramento to Cape Horn — Silver Mining — Among the Snow-Sheds — Deserts and Indians — Great Salt Lake — The Sacred Inclosure — Tabernacle and Temple — The Lion House and the Beehive — A Thriving City — A Résumé of Mormon History — The Creed and Government of the Church — Fort Douglas........................ 181

XXVII. CROSSING THE ROCKY MOUNTAINS

PAGE

Wild and Grand Scenery — New and Wonderful Hot Springs — Six Hundred Miles for Twenty-five Cents — Two Miles up in the Air — Leadville, Colorado — The Collegiate Mountains — Climbing Marshall Pass — Railroads as High as Mount Blanc — Engines play Hide and Seek — The Royal Gorge — An Engineering Feat — The Pittsburgh of the West ........................................ 192

XXVIII. COLORADO SPRINGS, MANITOU, AND DENVER

The Invalids' Home — The Mineral Springs of Manitou — "Garden of the Gods" — Helen Hunt Jackson's Grave — Pike's Peak — Its Difficulties, Wonders, and Glories — The Central City of the Union — Mines and Industries — Enterprising People — Daniel Webster no Prophet — The View from City Park — Hospitality and Home Feeling — On to the Exposition — Home Again ........................ 204

# LIST OF ILLUSTRATIONS.

|  |  |
|---|---|
| AN AVENUE IN SOUTHERN CALIFORNIA | *Frontispiece* |
| | FACING PAGE |
| THE LEVEE, NEW ORLEANS | 8 |
| THE ALAMO, SAN ANTONIO | 20 |
| INDIAN GROUP, ARIZONA | 30 |
| CALIFORNIA ROSE GARDEN | 50 |
| RAMONA'S MARRIAGE PLACE, SAN DIEGO | 58 |
| PASADENA AND MOUNT WILSON | 66 |
| ROSE COTTAGE, LOS ANGELES | 78 |
| SANTA BARBARA | 82 |
| CASTLE ROCK, SANTA BARBARA BAY | 86 |
| BELFRY OF SAN GABRIEL MISSION | 90 |
| FLOWER FESTIVAL, SANTA BARBARA | 96 |
| OLIVE GROVE, COOPER'S RANCH | 104 |
| OAK GROVE, NEAR GAVIOTA | 108 |
| OLD ADOBE, SANTA BARBARA | 112 |
| YOSEMITE VALLEY FROM UNION POINT | 118 |
| BRIDAL VEIL FALL, YOSEMITE | 126 |
| BIG TREES, SANTA CRUZ | 132 |
| CYPRESS GROUP, MONTEREY | 154 |
| LICK OBSERVATORY, MOUNT HAMILTON | 164 |
| ROUNDING CAPE HORN, SIERRA NEVADA | 182 |
| CASTLE GATE, ROCKY MOUNTAINS | 192 |
| PIKE'S PEAK FROM COLORADO SPRINGS | 204 |

*\*\** *The thanks of the Publishers are due Messrs. W. H. Jackson Co. of Denver, Taber of San Francisco, and Watkins of San Francisco for the use of photographs from which the illustrations in this book are made.*

# BEYOND THE ROCKIES

## I

### SOUTH AND WEST

FROM WINTER TO SPRING — PLANS FOR MEXICO NIPPED IN THE BUD — A RAYMOND EXCURSION — VIRGINIA AND TENNESSEE — LOOKOUT MOUNTAIN — ITS SCENES AND MEMORIES

THE streets of New York were piled high with snow, and a bitter winter wind, which had been blowing for the greater part of three months, made our bones ache and our throats sore. The memories of the Riviera, and Tangier, and Malaga began to assert themselves, and the temptation to go by the new Mediterranean route to a land of sun and warmth was very strong. Yet we remembered the oft-repeated question when in Spain: "You have been in Mexico?" and the assertion made by an enthusiastic traveller, that Mexico was better worth seeing than Spain, and that California as far surpassed the Riviera as the garden of Eden excelled the Central Park. Let us go to Mexico, and come home by California and the Chicago Fair. So plans were made, and tickets were engaged, and March was to come in like a lion, and drive us out to pastures new and green.

When all was ready, the trunks packed, and the key in the door, that friend and foe of travellers, the electric telegraph, brought word that there was an epidemic of typhus fever in Mexico, and that it would be risky to make the tour. We sadly laid aside Prescott's "Conquest of Mexico" and the other interesting volumes with which we had been refreshing our minds, and had nearly laid aside the carefully planned route through California, and determined to see the winter out, if it took all summer to do it. But wiser counsels prevailed, and we turned the key in the lock, spent two hours in driving over frozen billows of mud and snow to the Central Railroad station at the foot of Liberty Street, and took places in a Pullman car, which was to be our bed by night and boudoir by day, for a pull across the continent.

All experienced travellers had advised us not to travel in Mexico without having a dining-car in the train, and to secure that needful comfort we had joined what is known as a "Raymond" party. This is a conducted party of tourists who travel in a more elegant and comfortable manner than the ordinary parties with which the travelling public is familiar. They have their own train, not crowded or commonplace, they go according to their own schedules, and have all the luxuries which can be furnished on the route at their command. If the hotels are poor, they use their own hotel, which is always first-class, and their tickets and luggage and everything else which impede and irritate the ordinary traveller, are cared for by experienced and agreeable attendants. This is the theory of a "Raymond" excursion, and I am bound to say that, allowance being made for the accidents of existence, and the frailty of human nature under the best circumstances, the practice accords fairly well with the theory. Some things will not always work harmoniously, and it so happened that the Boston part of the train was delayed by a "lost Pullman," and by heavy snowdrifts, so that the New Yorkers waited five hours in Philadelphia for the "slow coaches" from New England. There is a calm and serene atmosphere about the City of Brotherly Love which tends to reduce irritation and lessen impatience, and so we welcomed our belated friends with a smile, and dined together in unity as we steamed on to Washington. Night found us in the Shenandoah Valley, and morning dawned upon us near the Natural Bridge. All traces of snow were gone. The tender blades of grass were just pushing through the earth, the clear air was resonant with the songs of birds, and the rivers ran full and yellow with the unfrosted and crumbling soil. It was a great and beneficent change from icy winter to the breath of early spring.

Through the day we journeyed on through Virginia and Eastern Tennessee, spending an hour at Bristol, which has the characteristics of a border town between two states, groups of tall, lean, broad-shouldered men lounging at corners, and rows of well-splashed horses hitched in front of the main avenue stores, while the trolley cars hissed and rocked along the uneven track in the street. The churches were the best buildings in the place. A few handsome houses on the bluff gave evidence of wealth and prosperity, while crowds of poorly clad negro boys, loafing and loitering in the sunshine, formed another element in the picture. At Morristown we came to the familiar scenery of the road leading through the Balsams into the Asheville Valley, where we spent some pleasant weeks just a year before, and then we came to Knoxville, the large, thriving, and growing town, which has one of the longest and most honorable histories — civil, military, and religious — of the towns in this region. We had elected to pass by Knoxville, and to run to Chattanooga, and find our first stopping-place on the summit of Lookout Mountain, at the Lookout Mountain Inn, a new and elaborate establishment in one of the grandest positions of the country. The building is new, and is placed on the eastern face of the mountain. It has a fine frontage of three hundred and sixty-five feet, fully cleared, which commands an unsurpassed view over the valley of the Tennessee, and is flanked on either side by forests of oak and pine. In the winter the air is clear and mild, and the heats of summer are tempered by cool breezes which play over the lofty mountain height. Rising seven hundred feet above the valley in which the city of Chattanooga lies, and twenty-two hundred feet above the sea-level, with precipitous sides, it affords views of exceptional grandeur and extent, and the panorama is remarkable for variety and beauty. From this summit, portions of seven states can be seen, and here are some of the most famous battle-fields of the Civil War. Far to the northwest, the blue outlines of the Cumberland Mountains line the horizon, while a multitude of lower peaks rise nearer in the landscape. On the east lie Walden's Ridge and Sherman Heights, and then comes the famous Missionary Ridge, backed by the Great Smokies which have been made famous by the romances of Charles Egbert Craddock. In front, the Tennessee River sweeps in wide curves through a vast semicircular plain, and the populous and busy town, with its converging lines of railroad, is spread out as on a map before the eye.

One is reminded here of Sherman, and Thomas, and Grant, and Hooker; of the battles of Missionary Ridge and Chickamauga, and of the terrible struggle which has passed into history as "the battle above the clouds." An old Confederate soldier acts as guide to the tourist, and there are few of the struggles of the Rebellion which have such a vantage ground from which their movements can be pointed out and described to the visitor of to-day. Lookout Mountain extends over the border-line into Georgia, and along its rugged sides are points of observation, each revealing wonderful views and manifold attractions of woodland, water, and mountain scenery. Two railroads climb the summit, one by a series of zigzags which in ten miles moves four times across the face of the cliffs, rising each time about four hundred feet; the other is a cable road which ascends directly from the valley up a steep incline. A fine carriage road also brings the traveller up in an hour, and connects with many excellent drives over the country.

Far in the distance is seen the National Cemetery, where, among costly and elegant monuments, lie four thousand unknown dead whose graves are marked by a single white stone, the memorials of a conflict which, unlike most civil wars, has bound a people more strongly than ever in national unity. Long may it be before this broad and heaven-blessed land shall again be bathed in blood! Mutual self-respect, honor, justice, and the nobility of the American people are among the heritages of those years of war; have they not also taught us the value of mutual forbearance, national patriotism, and Christian love and labor, to make a nation great?

## II

## FROM THE MOUNTAINS TO THE GULF

BIRMINGHAM AND ITS ACTIVITIES — SPRING IN NEW ORLEANS — BEAUTY AND BUSINESS — THE LOUISIANA LOTTERY — GROWTH, ENTERPRISE, AND PROSPERITY — DR. PALMER AND HIS CHURCH

FROM Lookout Mountain, with its picturesque scenery and historic reminiscences, to the practical and modern city of Birmingham, Alabama, is a great change, but a ride of a few hours on the famous Queen and Crescent Railway effected the transformation. Spring had not clothed the earth with fresh garments, but here and there a peach tree bloomed pink, and the white blossoms of the spiræa waved in the mild breeze. Some ploughing had been done, but for the most part all things in nature were awaiting the touch of the enchanter to burst forth in vernal loveliness. Birmingham, however, was all alive. Its electric cars hissed along wide avenues, hurling crowds of people through the town, and making the air resonant with gongs and the whirr of wheels. A mad "dummy" engine with two open cars, wildly tossing and heaving as if upon mid-ocean, plunged up and down hill and valley, through town and suburb, with tolling bell and shrieking whistle, the load of passengers constantly changing; and the sidewalks were full of people, hurrying hither and thither as if a section of Chicago had been let loose in this Alabama town. There were new buildings since a year ago, and more were being built, and it seemed as if we were in a paradise of "drummers," and a place whence rest and quiet had forever fled. It were better to sleep on the rumbling train, which seemed slow beside this fast town, and so the rising sun found us in the middle of Lake Pontchartrain, seven miles of which are crossed by this railway on a bridge of piles before entering the city of New Orleans.

When I was in New Orleans just a year before, a bitter "norther" had swooped down upon the city, frozen the strawberries into bullets, and cut down all the flowers and early vegetables. Under such circumstances it was not easy to believe that March was anything but a roaring lion, whether encountered on Boston Common or on the Mississippi Levee. This year, I am assured, the spring is normal, and it is a very lovely season. The gardens and dooryards of the handsome villas on St. Charles Avenue and Prytania Street were full of roses, climbing over arches, clinging to trellises, and gathered into masses of color here and there on the green lawns; beds of hyacinths and lilies, acacia with its yellow hair, and the wax-like china-berry, blooming amidst palms and oleanders; the fresh green foliage of the liveoaks and the polished dark leaves of the magnolia delighted the eye and filled the air with fragrance. Our days were spent in the

THE LEVEE, NEW ORLEANS

open, and with the blossoming spring the population seemed to have a new character. Bright colors flowed along the avenues as crowds of beautiful women and girls, happy and laughing, gathered on the promenades to shop, to chatter, to see, and to be seen. Even the men had caught the tone of the season, and for one black coat there were a dozen gray or fawn-colored, and a flood of sunshine filled the streets and sparkled all over the laughing waves of the red and rushing rivers. The levees were loaded with bales of cotton and boxes of sugar and barrels of turpentine and rice, and great vessels were discharging as well as loading cargoes.

There was a drawing of the Louisiana Lottery while we were in the city. Its days in Louisiana and in the United States are numbered, and it will be no longer a blot and a disgrace to American civilization, though I fear that it will still reap from its new rendezvous in Honduras a harvest of victims from our country. It is a sad fact that, while the lottery has been established in the South, it has been largely supported by the North. At the recent drawing, the capital prize was drawn in Boston, and many of the other large prizes were drawn in such cities as Cleveland, and Rochester, and Detroit. The passion for gambling is not confined by isothermal lines, and rages as furiously in the staid and pious state of New Jersey as among the Creoles of the Gulf of Mexico. Great credit is due to the state of Louisiana for ridding itself from the evil monster that injured its reputation and its own people, while enticing others to sin. This state is growing steadily in those elements of character and conduct which make political communities strong and great. The city problem here, as elsewhere, is a hard one to solve, but there is much salt in New Orleans, and with the outgoing of the lottery one bad thing will pass away. Some persons may imagine that the drawings of the lottery are scenes of excitement, but nothing could be farther from the truth. They are as formal and businesslike as the announcement of the prizes at a college commencement, and not half as interesting as an auction sale. They take place in the Opera House, and are attended by a moderate audience. Upon a platform are two large wheels, in one of which are the numbers, amounting to hundreds of thousands. These numbers are inclosed in little gutta-percha tubes. In the other wheel are similar tubes containing the various numbers of dollars which constitute the prizes. Thus, while there may be three hundred thousand tickets sold or given out for sale at a drawing, there are only eleven hundred and thirty-six prizes, varying from seventy-five thousand to forty dollars. General Early, the Confederate general, sat beside one wheel; another man, who has taken the place of General Beauregard since his death, sat at the other wheel. Two negro boys, blindfolded, stood between the two, and in the rear, at a table, were clerks to record the drawings. After a brief announcement of what drawing was to be made, by General Early, in a thin and tremulous voice, the wheels were turned by an assistant, and opened. The blinded boy put his hand in and took out one of the gutta-percha tubes. It was broken open by General Early, and the number called. We will say that it was 11,271. The other boy put his hand into the other wheel, drew out a tube, and handed it to the representative of General Beauregard. He broke the tube and read out three hundred dollars. This result he announced, and a record was made on the blackboard for all to see that No. 11,271 had drawn the prize of three hundred dollars. The paper number and the paper bearing the dollar marks were then fastened together, and passed to the registering clerks. All this was done rapidly and mechanically, from eight to twelve numbers being called in a minute. Now and then a request was made to turn the wheel. Then it was closed up, and a strong man came forward and gave the great circle a few turns, after which it was opened again, and the drawing went forward as before. It took several hours to draw the eleven hundred and thirty-six prizes. Of course, all the rest of the numbers remaining in the wheel failed to win, and were summarily destroyed, and with them the hopes of hundreds of thousands of men and women who had bought tickets. Few are aware of the length to which this gambling mania has extended, though most pastors and physicians know some of its sad results. I knew one man of good reputation, a thrifty farmer, who was ruined by drawing a prize of fifteen thousand dollars. Work had no more charms for him; he idled and gambled away his time and money, and died a sot. I knew a reputable and respected physician who spent most of the earnings of a large practice in the Louisiana

Lottery, and left his family without a dollar, and no one ever imagined how he could have made such poor investments! The number of clerks who have defrauded their employers, and business men who failed through the temptations of the lottery, would make a long, sad list. Let us be thankful that if the serpent is not killed, he will at least be scotched.

I said that there was steady growth in good and strong elements in Louisiana. This is evident in the many sound and valuable enterprises which are set on foot in the state, its increase of railroad-building, farming, and manufacturing, and also in the enlargement and support of literary and religious associations, schools, and churches. The Southern people have a religious nature that responds to culture, and while there is a class that find pleasure and excitement in the race course, the prize ring, and kindred sports, these are not the representative people any more than they are elsewhere. In the closely seated pews of the First Presbyterian Church in Lafayette Square on Sunday morning, when I heard the venerable, but still strong, Dr. Palmer preach an old-fashioned gospel sermon, eloquent, powerful, and with pathetic appeal, I recognized the saving element of such a city as New Orleans. There was nothing sensational in the sermon, except as truth vividly presented and clearly defined and earnestly enforced is sensational. Dr. Palmer stood upon the platform, and spoke like an orator possessed and mastered by his theme, and the audience listened intently for nearly an hour with no sign of restlessness or satiety. When the sermon was ended, his assistant made a short prayer, and after a single verse sung with full organ and by all the people, the congregation, numbering from fifteen hundred to two thousand people, streamed out into the square, and went homeward in every direction.

# III

## ALONG THE SUNSET ROAD

LOUISIANA AND ITS FERTILE ACRES — BAYOUS AND RICE-FIELDS — GALVESTON AND ITS BEACH — HOUSTON AND ITS BOOM — LITERARY CURIOSITIES

FROM New Orleans our course lay through the southern portion of Louisiana. A large ferry-boat takes the heavy Pullman train across the Mississippi River to the station of the Southern Pacific Railroad at Algiers. Great neatness and taste are shown here, as also at all the road stations. Vines grow over the buildings, and these stand in gardens of semi-tropical trees and flowers. Through a well-cultivated region, we come to the swamps where alligators find their home, then to rice-fields, frequently crossing broad bayous and mouths of the Mississippi. Evidences of prosperity and profitable agriculture are all about us. The lands of Louisiana yield under cultivation from twenty-five to fifty bushels of corn, from one to three hogsheads of sugar, per acre, and one or two bales of cotton. Rice yields thirty to seventy-five bushels to the acre, and is planted broadcast in the lowlands, but in the highlands it is sown in rows, and cultivated with the plough, being cut by machinery and threshed like our wheat.

The sugar interests are very extensive, and absorb a great amount of capital. I was most agreeably disappointed at the fertility and excellent cultivation which the ride through Louisiana exhibited. Evidences of thrift and industry were manifest everywhere, in well-tilled farms, new and well-kept buildings, and enterprise along the bayous and at shipping ports. The scenery is varied and attractive, and the journey to Texas one of the pleasantest portions of our trip. The "Sunset" route leads through Louisiana to the great state of Texas, the largest state in the Union, containing two hundred and seventy-four thousand square miles, and nearly two and a half millions of inhabitants. It is three times as large as the state of New York, and has a great variety of soil and climate. And here let me say that much allowance must be made for statements about climate. Nothing is more fickle and uncertain than weather, and few persons think alike about it. When, therefore, we read of regions where it is never too cold or too hot, where it never rains or blows, where earth is a paradise, and the heavens a beautiful canopy throughout the year, it will not do to accept these things literally.

During the days that we spent at New Orleans and in Louisiana the sun was bright, the air was mild and fragrant, all nature seemed to rejoice, and the city to be merry in the general joy; but when we had passed through the state of Louisiana, and come to Galveston, in Texas, it was almost winter. "What is the matter with the climate?" said I to the livery stable keeper as I ordered a carriage to drive upon the magnificent beach. His reply illustrates my remarks. "It was splendid weather yesterday, but a 'blue norther' came down last night and froze us out." Before I had driven an hour on the beach I was as cold as ever I got in the great New York blizzard, though there was no sign of frost nor flake of snow.

Galveston is a prosperous town on the Gulf of Mexico, with several tributary railroads, and a large importing and exporting business. Its large and extensive warehouses, and stores of brick and stone, and many elegant residences sit on the sides and corners of wide streets laid out at right angles in the deep sand, through which the horses drag their heavy loads. One paved avenue gives access to the beach, which is one of the finest in the world, extending for forty miles along the Gulf of Mexico, hard, smooth, of the finest white sand, and so gradual in its slope as to render it a safe thoroughfare at all times of wind and tide. At some points there are clusters of summer houses with accommodations for bathing, and a large hotel connected with Galveston by an electric railroad invites the resident as well as the traveller to the seashore and its delights. The landlord said that it was never too hot for pleasure there, because of the cool airs from the Gulf, but when I asked him whether it was never too cool for comfort, he admitted that the steam-pipes in the dining-room and the big stove in the hall were arranged in view of the not unfrequent invasion of these mild shores by the "blue norther" during the winter season. The gardens in Galveston had some palm trees and manifold flowers growing in them, and the place was attractive and pleasant with a few exceptional features. The deep sand in the streets, the hissing trolley roads, and the electric lights which destroy the eyesight, are the disagreeable things in an otherwise most agreeable town. The inhabitants are well-to-do, thrifty, hospitable, and intelligent, as all their works and ways most certainly prove.

We spent an afternoon at Houston. A greater contrast could hardly be imagined than between Houston and Galveston. I have described Galveston. Houston is its opposite. It stands upon hills. Its streets are dirty, unpaved, rough, and stony. Bar-rooms abound; filthy, unkempt, and drunken men loaf about the corners and swarm at the liquor shops. Twelve lines of electric cars make travel noisy and dangerous. Jaded beasts and rattletrap wagons are drawn up at well-gnawed hitching-posts. The shops are full of coarse and tawdry goods, and the air is redolent of vile smells, and blue with profanity and tobacco smoke. Upon a hill several miles from Houston, under the name of Houston Heights, another city is being erected.

It is two miles from the Harris County courthouse in Houston to the Houston Heights Grand Boulevard, and thence the route of the electric cars lies through the new town. Graded and paved and sewered streets, supplied with water and electricity, have been laid out through the forest upon the heights. Specimen houses have been built, and lots are for sale "at rates that defy competition," as the cheap clothing stores say in their advertisements. Fine stone and lumber, as well as sand, are close at hand, and if I lived in Houston I should not delay a single day in moving out to the new town. There are several cities which have been recommended to me by interested parties as desirable places to make investments, but I certainly would not advise my friends to bury their earnings in any town lots which they do not know more about than I can tell them about the plant and power of this new city. Texas is a large state, and there is much land in it to be possessed. It is a rude state, albeit a powerful and independent one. Its people fought for their independence, and value it, and assert it in ways which are not always agreeable to mild-mannered people, and which contact with civilization will modify and probably improve. The gospel of cleanliness, and decent speech, and politeness, which obtains through the old Southern states equally with the North, has not spread completely over the "Lone Star," and the language of comment and criticism, as used in the daily press, does not indicate a high degree of intellectual or moral culture.

## IV

## SAN ANTONIO DE BEXAR

THE BORDER FORTRESS — A THRILLING HISTORY — THE ALAMO AND ITS DEFENDERS — SCENES IN THE TOWN — THE JESUIT MISSIONS — A GOVERNMENT POST AND EVENING PARADE

A JOURNEY of nearly six hundred miles from New Orleans brings the traveller to the large and interesting city of San Antonio de Bexar (pronounced *Vayhar*, and usually known as San Antonio), which has about fifty thousand inhabitants, a thrilling history, and an active and prosperous present. Here the old Spanish and priestly rule is represented by ruined missions and churches; the Mexican occupation is still kept in mind by that quarter of the town inhabited by the black-haired, yellow race, with bead eyes, piercing and restless. There they continue their ancient customs, and eat their open-air suppers of tortillas at midnight on the plaza. But the restless and aggressive Anglo-Saxon, with his intensely practical civilization, has made a show of the Alamo, put trolley roads through all the avenues, built new and elegant stone banks and public edifices for municipal and government offices, and established one of the largest and best appointed military posts upon the continent. In a few years the Spanish and Mexican character of the place will have passed away, and American railroad and business enterprise will have changed the romantic and historic town into a thriving and busy modern city. At present one can wander through the old missions, and think of the struggles of the Jesuit fathers, hear from the guide who lived through the epoch the story of how the Alamo, the fortified mission of the Franciscan monks, was lost and won, when Davy Crockett, and Colonel Bowie, and Colonel Travis, with one hundred and forty-seven other heroes, laid down their lives in the old church, after killing and wounding in their desperate defence more than six times their own number; and easily trace the progress of events which made the Mexican province and the republic of Texas a state in the great and powerful Federal Union. The best historical sketch of San Antonio was written by Sidney Lanier in 1872, and it includes in its finished narrative many things which had never been grouped before.

San Antonio de Bexar was founded in 1712, and four years later the Franciscan fathers began to build their missions. Controversies with the French, who owned and occupied Louisiana, continued for many years, but the Spanish rule was arbitrary and severe. In 1744 the present church of the Alamo was built, and the colonists and missionaries led a struggling existence for nearly half a century more. Father Marest had declared, in 1712, that the conversion of the Indians was "a miracle of the Lord's mercy, and that it was necessary first to

THE ALAMO, SAN ANTONIO

transform them into men, and afterward to labor to make them Christians." Massacres and experience of bitter cruelties had taught them, as they have taught other missionaries since, that the quality of mercy has no place in the natural heart of the American Indian.

Years of warfare between Indians, Spanish, Mexicans, and Americans followed, culminating in the massacre, of which mention has been made, in 1836. Then came a brief period of independence, and finally the annexation of Texas, in 1845, to the United States, since which time its progress has been rapid in everything which makes a state powerful and prosperous.

San Antonio covers a large territory. The business portion is closely built in every conceivable style of architecture. An elegant bank building of carved stone adjoins a dilapidated frame structure, and handsome brick stores are flanked by sheds and shanties or houses of sun-dried bricks. The main square, on which stand the post-office, the Merger Hotel, and the ruins of the Alamo Mission, has a small park, with trees and flowers in its centre; and the square upon which the cathedral and the municipal building stand is broad and handsome; but most of the business streets are narrow, ill paved, and pervaded by the obnoxious trolley. The residential quarters occupy broad and shaded avenues, where one and two story wooden houses stand embowered in fragrant vines and trees, with an air of comfort and rural quiet strangely contrasting with the central district. Here the rich and hospitable inhabitants live and entertain their guests in the midst of semi-tropical delights, for the climate of the place is agreeable in winter, and not unhealthy though hot in summer.

Upon a rolling plateau north of the town is the Government Post, one of the largest in the United States, containing, however, at present, only about six companies of troops, several thousand of the men being on duty along the Mexican border. There are two parade grounds, each surrounded by extensive barracks and well-built officers' quarters, and a feature of the military life is the dress parade and military drills which are constantly taking place. The new post occupies one hundred and sixty-two acres, and the main buildings surround a quadrangle six hundred and twenty-four feet square, with a lofty tower in the centre, from which a fine view of the town, with the meandering river on its way to the Gulf, is obtained. When the sun was westering, we drove to the hill and saw the troops parade, their flag still draped in black in token of respect to the soldier President, R. B. Hayes, then recently deceased. It was good in this outpost of our country to see the discipline and drill of the American soldier, and to know that though our army is only a little nucleus of thoroughly trained men, yet it represents a force of millions of patriotic citizens which could be mobilized for defence at brief notice, — men who have the courage, the capacity, and much of the training which combine to make efficient soldiers. While the memories of the war of the Rebellion last, there will not be wanting brave and able defenders of the American Union. Many distinguished men have held command and served at San Antonio, whose lives and doings form a part of history larger than the department. They have worn the blue and the gray uniform, but their devotion to military duty, whether on the field of battle in the gaze of thousands, or grappling with a redskin in the mesquite wilderness, none may question. They have guarded our Southern frontier, and aided by a gallant population have settled the Indian question in Texas. San Antonio in the past has had a rough and bloody record; it seems now to have entered upon the piping times of peace, and an era of prosperity which its struggles and effort well deserve.

There are many places about the town which will interest the tourist. We drove two miles or more along a pleasant road, between market gardens fed with water by a long *acequia*, to the Mission of the Concepcion. The old church, with its quaint gray towers and high-walled dome in the rear, is a very respectable ruin, with many of its frescoes still visible, and its corridors and windows yet remaining, and abundantly supplied with the thorny cactus as a hindrance to the artist and the relic hunter. Further down the river a couple of miles, is the Mission of San José de Aguayo. These buildings are in good repair, and regular services are held here, while six miles further on is the San Juan Mission, now little more than a heap of ruins. Resting in these ruined buildings, one can dream of the conquests of Spain in the New World, and reflect upon the wonderful Providence which has brought so many of these strongholds of superstition under the powerful influence of a purer faith.

## V

## ALONG THE RIO GRANDE

WILD AND PICTURESQUE SCENERY — THE TOWN OF LANGTRY — A ONE-MAN GOVERNMENT — DESERT VIEWS — MARATHON AND ITS GREEKS — TIME AT EL PASO

FOUR miles west of Del Rio, on the Southern Pacific Railroad, the tourist catches the first glimpse of the Rio Grande del Norte, and three miles farther on is the beginning of the Grand Cañon, on the bank of the romantic river which geographically separates Mexico and the United States. Wild gorges between huge piles of limestone rocks, deep valleys intersecting one another, queer conical hills and vast amphitheatres succeed each other, and far below the winding railroad track, the yellow waters of the river combine to form pictures of beauty and grandeur which offer great attractions to the traveller. In one of the wildest portions of the route, the train halts to allow the passengers to climb into the "painted cave," where curious deposits of limestone, shells, and fossils, and flints abound, where I gathered delicate maidenhair ferns and flowers, and from which the view is superb. The cave is not a hole in the ground, but a concavity in the mountain side, from which one looks across the chasm where the river runs, and into a vast circular amphitheatre in the distance, directly in front of the cave and scooped out of the surrounding mountains. Seated in this concave one could imagine the performance by giants and genii of some colossal dramatic spectacle, or grander yet, the assembly of a nation as at Sinai to hear the solemn announcement of the law of God. The air was pure and dry, and the voice could be heard for a long distance, but no human assembly of which there is any record has ever been gathered here. The East with its holy places will ever be the goal of the cultivated and reverential student, while the natural wonders of the Western Continent will inspire the imagination and delight the senses of the sentimental and enthusiastic traveller. Beyond this cave the mouth of the Devil's River is reached, and over a fine iron bridge of five spans of one hundred and fifty feet each the railway crosses, and continues to climb along the mountain and river side.

For a considerable distance the road maintains a lofty elevation on the bank of the Rio Grande, the soil being dry and unfertile, till the town of Langtry is reached. This town consists of one shanty, over the door of which is painted "Jersey Lily." Within was a single room, with a rude bar, a table covered with empty whiskey bottles, a pile of bone "chips" for poker-playing, and some stray playing-cards. Several bottles had pieces of guttered candles stuck in the cork-hole, and there was an odor of stale tobacco about the room. One man owns this township, and is mayor, alderman, and chief of police all in one. His methods of civil government, if they may be judged by what lay around in the city hall, are not very different from those of larger cities with which we are familiar.

Most of the towns along the railroad are mere names on paper, and water-tank stations. At Sanderson, we found a neat and good store, an establishment for rearing pug dogs, which seemed to be thriving, and a school of five girls and one boy with a sore face. All were very dirty and slovenly, and the pale and hollow-eyed teacher, who was not much cleaner than her pupils, excused the dirt and disorder because there had been no rain for five months. Everything was dusty and dry, and there were no signs of water except at the railway tank.

Vast circles of limestone hills were covered with clumps of dry bushes and hundreds of dagger plants, their central flowers of creamy white surrounded by green fronds spiked at the end; and in some valleys there was a short, fine grass plentifully mixed with manifold and beautiful flowers. The sky was clear, the air warm and pure, the landscape gray and monotonous in the extreme. As we rode along, one plain succeeded another, and one amphitheatre of hills opened into another; sometimes cattle were browsing where there was seemingly nothing to eat, but the cattle, and mules, and horses, and pigs that we saw all looked fat and healthy. Sometimes we passed hours without any signs of life; no birds even hovered over the desert region. Then, suddenly, herds of cattle would appear, and these almost always indicated the presence of wells or pools of

water. At one place there was a small menagerie;
a bear, a Mexican lion, an eagle, and a coyote were
in rough cages; and to amuse the passengers the
bear was put through his programme of tricks. The
road continued to rise, and the heavy breathing of
the engine gave proof of the steepness of the grade.
We passed "Longfellow" and "Emerson" without
knowing it, but at "Marathon" we halted. The
inhabitants looked very much like ancient Greeks,
both in respect to the tawny color of their skin, and
the number of weapons which they carried, but we
did not stay to hear the news of any modern Thermopylæ. Still climbing, we reached the highest
point on the Sunset route, at Paisano, a point about
two hundred miles east of El Paso. This is also
the highest along the entire route between New
Orleans and San Francisco, being 5082 feet above
the level of the sea. The air is dry and rarefied at
this place, and one's breathing was perceptibly
quickened. At Langtry our elevation had been
1320 feet, and from Paisano we went down to a level
of 3713 feet, on which the town of El Paso is built.
The Rio Grande is seen again here, and can be crossed
by several bridges, but it is already, in this month
of March, a dwindling and rapidly drying stream.
El Paso stands at the junction of Texas, Mexico,
and New Mexico. It is a large town with handsome
public buildings, streets of shops, and many finelooking churches. It stands upon an extensive
plain, and circles of mountains appear in the distance. These peaks do not seem to belong to any
main chain, but are huge, disjointed ridges scattered

all over the country, and look like black icebergs floating in a light gray sea. Their outlines are rough and jagged, their sides are serrated; at sunset they are bathed in violet light, and resemble the mountains of Greece. Sometimes they form a feature in the desert mirage, and seem to be islands in mid-ocean, anon grouped and connected in a vast mountain range, like the ramparts of the Rocky Mountains. Then the mists will melt away, and as grim sentinels they will march off, each to his separate station. No part of the journey across the continent can compare, for variety and magic of scenery, with these sunsets upon the desert regions of New Mexico and Arizona. The atmosphere is so rare and clear, the effects of light and shade are so strange, and the coloring of earth and vegetation, of rock and sky, is so peculiar, that the general effect is picturesque, and at the same time entirely unlike anything to be seen elsewhere. El Paso is the place where time changes. Mr. Johnston says that they used to have at El Paso, an Eastern, Western, Northern, and Southern time, a mountain, railroad, local, Mexican, and mean time; and not being satisfied with these, some one — probably of Aztec origin — actually proposed having a sun time. "They had so many hands on the town clock that a strike seemed imminent at every hour. This state of things was confusing to strangers; they made all sorts of mistakes. A strange traveller, westbound, went to bed one night at 9 P.M. by one clock and got up at 6 A.M. by another, and only had two hours to rest. He paid his bill on Eastern time, and thereby saved his dinner. He managed to catch the east and westbound trains both at one time, and finally found himself a hundred miles south in Mexico, and it took a mathematician, a watchmaker, and an old sailor several hours to straighten him out." All this is changed now. The time is moved two hours back to San Francisco time when going west, and two hours forward to New Orleans time when going east. Of course the time is arbitrary, but arbitrary measures are better than uncertainty, and in the matter of time it is of great importance to know what to expect.

# VI

## NEW MEXICO AND ARIZONA

THE TOWN OF JUARES — OVER THE BORDER — CLIMATE AND HEALTH — INDIAN VILLAGES — SUNDAY AT TUCSON — ITS SCHOOLS AND UNIVERSITY

BEFORE leaving El Paso, we crossed the Rio Grande into Mexico. There can be no greater change than from the busy American town in Texas, with its railroad activity and the civilization of the nineteenth century making itself visible everywhere, to the mediæval Spanish, Mexican, Indian village of Juares, which lies across the river. The only modern thing that enters the village is a street-car from El Paso, and this is drawn by a single mule, has Spanish lettering on its sides, and is visited on every trip by a custom-house officer, who either makes a profound bow or invites the passenger to go with him to the court, according to his temper and condition. Two youths who offended his majesty by wearing back from Juares to El Paso gorgeously trimmed Mexican sombreros, were marched off to the justice, and paid fifty-five per cent duty for their fun, while a venerable old gentleman whose pockets were stuffed with Vera Cruz cigars received only a polite bow and a free

INDIAN GROUP, ARIZONA

pass. Once in Juares, and one might fancy himself in the middle of Mexico, or even in some parts of old Spain. Black-haired, tawny-skinned, keen-eyed men, with leather leggings, and gay shawls over their shoulders, and broad-brimmed, conical straw and felt hats on their heads, lounged under the scanty foliage of trees that seemed dying for want of water; withered beggars danced and whined, "For the love of God give us something;" the dust was white and deep, the walls were whitewashed, the houses were of adobe, — sun-dried bricks a foot square, — and the shops were little coops in which the tradesmen sat and worked or bartered, much as they do to-day in Tangier and Fez, or as they used to do forty years ago in Cairo and Damascus. There is an old church, with a tawdry image of the Virgin and some wretched altar trimmings, built a couple of hundred years ago, which contains richly carved roof-beams, between which is an ingenious network of small round poles arranged in a neat pattern. The houses are all of adobe, and of one story. This sun-dried mud makes a cool and dry house, and if it is protected from water at the foundation, and at the top by a projecting roof, it is an excellent structure, cool at midday and warm at midnight, and well suited to a climate where rain falls rarely and never for a long time.

The climate of El Paso is not unlike that of New Mexico, upon whose border-line it stands. The rainfall is slight, and irrigation is needful in order to raise anything; but water will make any part of this desert to bud and blossom and yield abundantly. The railroads have made the town important; for here the Denver and Rio Grande comes in, and the International line enters Mexico, while the Southern Pacific runs through from New Orleans to San Francisco. Our stay was pleasant, though brief, for the day was calm and warm, and the experiences were novel. The general appearance of the place is uninviting. As a health resort, the altitude and dryness of air would be great recommendations in some cases. Upon the other hand, when the wind blows, the fine dust and sand whirl about in clouds and penetrate everywhere through crack and crevice. There is a variety of churches, all well built, and the place has an air of active and healthy business.

We cut across a corner of New Mexico in pursuing our route. The territory has high mountain ranges, among which lie fertile valleys and lofty table-lands. The climate is dry, the rainfall slight, and in order to successful agriculture, the land must be plentifully irrigated. There are many mining industries here, and ranches for stock-raising. Cliff dwellings are found in some of the narrow valleys. They are stone structures lodged upon a shelf of rock, with an entrance from the top, and served as places of defence, as well as dwellings.

The Pueblo Indian villages are built of a number of adobe houses grouped together. The first story has no openings except loop-holes. The second story is reached by ladders, which can be drawn up on to the terrace. Sometimes two or more stories are arranged in this way, and it was probably both for protection and to carry out the communistic ideas of these Indians that this construction was adopted. Coronado, three hundred years ago, reported finding in New Mexico "very excellent, good houses of three or four, or five lots high, wherein are good lodgings and high chambers with ladders instead of chairs, and certain cellars underground very good and paved"; and the style of architecture has not changed since his time. A warm Sunday morning in March found us at Tucson (which is pronounced *Toosón*). The power of the sun made the shade of cottonwood trees grateful, even before breakfast, and by noon the whole region glowed with dry heat like a furnace. We found a cool place where the Sunday-school of the Congregational church was waiting for the teachers to come, and when the doors were opened, went in and joined in the service. From this religious assembly we drove over to the Indian school, and had a pleasant interview with the managers and teachers, of which we shall speak later. Tucson is a favorite resort for persons afflicted with lung troubles, but too stimulating for the majority of nervous invalids. The air is excessively dry and warm, being surrounded by hundreds of miles of uninhabited deserts and mountains, no snow ever falls, and the average number of days on which rain has fallen for a period of ten years is forty-two per year. One-half of these days were in midsummer, and the amount of rain was always small. The town lies twenty-five hundred feet above the sea-level, and the mountain scenery is grand and interesting, including lofty heights and deep cañons.

The game is not gone from this wild region. Quail and duck and deer are abundant in season, and there are wild animals within fifteen or twenty miles of the town. There is an old mission of San Xavier Del Bac about ten miles away, and it is not a ruin like most of these Spanish establishments. The successors of the old Padres still live there, and conduct services for their dwindling Mexican and Indian flock. The houses of the town are chiefly built of sun-dried brick, whitewashed upon the outside. A few are of red-burned brick, including most of the public buildings. The general appearance of the place is Mexican: the women wear the mantilla, and there are Indians with long, coarse black hair, often braided in tails or queues, and offering pottery and baskets for sale. These baskets are braided of willow and straw, and are so firm and close that water can be carried in them. For a sufferer from invalid lungs, there is no better place than this Arizona town. It is hot and dusty, the surrounding scenery is barren, and the advantages of society and culture are few; but there are Protestant churches and good schools, a conservatory of music, the Territorial University, and School of Mines, and many things to induce literary and benevolent effort. Persons of robust health, or those suffering from neuralgia, had better seek another home, and in our great country, with its varied climates and productions, there is a place for all sorts and conditions of men.

# VII

## ONE OF OUR INDIAN SCHOOLS

A PRESBYTERIAN CONTRACT — GOOD TEACHERS — THE CORRECT IDEA OF INDIAN EDUCATION — REPORTS FROM THE GOVERNMENT SUPERINTENDENT

WE spent a Sunday at Tucson, in Arizona, and accepted a polite invitation to visit the Indian Training School at that place. The buildings stand about half a mile from the town, and consist of a girls' home, a boys' home, a carpenter shop, laundry, and hospital. These have cost about twenty thousand dollars, and have been built by the Woman's Executive Committee of the Board of Home Missions of the Presbyterian Church. The Rev. Howard Billman has been for five years the superintendent, and under his direction all the buildings, except the girls' home, were built. He is assisted by his wife, who was matron for one year, and she now largely performs her husband's duties. Miss Pierson, of Philadelphia, a daughter of Rev. Arthur T. Pierson, D.D., Miss Ziegler, of Ohio, and Miss Timian, of New York, are the teachers in intellectual work. S. P. Pearson, of Lincoln, Nebraska, directs the carpenter work. The work on all of the buildings except the girls' home has been done by the boys under his supervision. There are five ladies regularly employed as instructors and officers in various departments of the household, and also a boys' matron, a farmer, and a supervisor. There were one hundred and thirty-eight Indian children at the time of our visit, of whom eighty were boys and fifty-eight girls, and fifty of these were over fourteen years of age. Last year there was an average of one hundred and fifty-two pupils, which crowded the buildings so that cots had to be placed in the school-rooms, and even now the school-rooms have to be used as sitting-rooms. The Indians are Pimas, Yûmas, and Papagoes, all quiet and peaceable tribes; the larger portion are from the last tribe, whose reservation is within nine miles of Tucson.

This school is a "contract" school. In the establishment of these schools, articles of agreement are entered into annually by the Commissioner of Indian Affairs and the officers of the Missionary Boards of various denominations. The government binds itself to pay one hundred and twenty-five dollars for the year, for each Indian child who is housed, fed, clothed, and taught according to the contract specifications. The government has the right to inspect the school, and to annul the contract if the board or mission fails to carry out its provisions. The government's aid and responsibility stop here. Those who establish the school must erect its buildings, provide the teachers, obtain the land for cultivation, farming implements, shops, tools, etc., and give training in the school-room on five days and industrial training on six days of each week, during ten months of the year. They have entire liberty in the management of the school, including authority to settle the amount and kind of religious instruction which shall be given. The superintendent of the Tucson school is a man of ideas and of great force of character, and this school is perhaps an exceptional institution. Certainly, the intelligence and aptitude displayed by the pupils would warrant the conclusion that they have been well taught. Mr. Billman aims to introduce the leaven of the Gospel among the people whose children are educated here — not a Gospel of words, but a Gospel that induces regeneration of heart and character in the individual, which makes men and women careful, industrious, and pure, useful members of the family, the community, and the state.

Mr. Billman says: "We take the Indian just as he is — uncleanly often, untaught, indolent, as poor as poverty can make him, and without backbone. It is possible for him to be clean, to be clothed, and to be fed. No one in this world owes him anything whatever, except to teach him how he can be a man and take care of himself. We are perfectly willing to expend strength of hands, and brain, and heart, in teaching him. We are not willing to do anything for him which he can do for himself, or to give him anything which he is able to get for himself. We believe that Indian children have rights. A command placed upon them is not simply an expression of the teacher's will, but an expression of what is right, what is suitable. They are carefully treated and nursed in sickness. The merchants of Tucson will bear witness that if there is any inferior article of food delivered for their consumption, it is not done with the knowledge of the management here. Bodily comfort is carefully considered in their clothing. Whatever they have beyond this, they are at liberty to get in any honorable way they can.

"The whole aim of our work is thus to send out a company of clean, industrious, self-respecting, self-reliant, self-supporting, and righteous Indians, who will till their lands, build homes for themselves, and live in enjoyment of the fruit of their toil. We shall be rejoiced if we can fit a few of the whole number to become teachers and evangelists; but we are no longer so vain as to hope that the first generation can be sufficiently educated to become successful lawyers, physicians, and ministers. Coming to us as children, utterly ignorant of our language, of our history and civilization, it is not possible in the time that they remain in school to give them an education that qualifies them for such callings. If we aim to send out a generation of Indians who shall endeavor to compete with the white men by living by its wits and not by toil, we shall be grievously disappointed. If we turn all our energy to the cultivation of industry, manliness, and independence, we may not realize all we hope for; but we shall realize enough to vindicate the wisdom of our methods."

These are sensible words, and Mr. Billman's experience with this Indian school, where industrial training is happily combined with mental culture, has shown the wisdom of such a course as he points out. Indians who are taught that manual labor is the lowest form of human work, are more ready than most men to accept the teaching and avoid the work. They soon lose the knowledge they held by a slight grasp, relapse into indolence and uncleanliness, and imitate the vices of civilization. Those, on the contrary, who are taught habits of industry and manual labor, become, in the course of time, useful and happy members of the communities where they live. Higher education may serve to help a selected number of Indians, as of other races, to a better than the common lot, but it still remains true for Indians, as for the rest of mankind, that the best and happiest condition is that in which daily toil furnishes occupation for mind and body, and the means of livelihood. In this connection it is gratifying to be able to quote a part of the report of Rev. Daniel Dorchester, then United States Superintendent of Indian Schools, upon the Tucson Indian Training School. Dr. Dorchester reports as follows: —

"SAN DIEGO, CAL., March 1, 1893.

"*To the Hon. Commissioner of Indian Affairs, Washington, D. C.:*

"SIR: I have the honor to report that I visited the Presbyterian Contract Indian School at Tucson, Arizona, February 3d and 4th. The school is under the superintendency of Rev. Howard Billman, who is now suffering from painful nervous prostration, the result of excessive labors in that enervating climate. Mr. Billman has had charge of the school from the beginning, or for about five years, and I regard it as one of the very best and most successful of the Indian contract schools. It has grown and improved much since my visit in March, 1890. From the beginning, the superintendent has been very fortunate in obtaining pupils. He has never been under the necessity of calling upon the Indian agent, the Indian police, or the district supervisor to bring children to his school. He has had more applications every year than he could accommodate — at the beginning of one year turning away more than fifty. The school buildings have been enlarged, doubling the accommodations of three years ago, and still applicants are turned away.

"The Tucson school has several advantages. It is quite near the homes of the Papagoes, their reservation being only nine miles away; and large numbers of the Papagoes are scattered in the regions adjacent and beyond the reservation. Tucson is the market where they trade, and they can conveniently see their children. This is a great point with Indians. The Indians have unbounded faith in Superintendent Billman. He is a wise and careful man, and has always been particular to fulfil his promises, gives the Indians good counsel, and helps them in many practical ways. Notwithstanding the Papagoes are Roman Catholics, and Mr. Billman is a Presbyterian, there has been no trouble between them over religious matters, but a strong mutual confidence. The school is very attractive, and its attraction is chiefly in the spirit of the superintendent and the employés — a kindly, wholesome atmosphere.

Some schools have more spectacular exercises, but this school attracts by its genuine Christian, intelligent, and kindly influence. Even discipline is administered in such a way as to strengthen the hold on the pupils.

"This school, from the beginning, has had a good class of teachers, among them the daughter of Rev. A. T. Pierson. Miss Pierson is particularly successful in object lesson methods, and possesses rare tact. Two of the present teachers are new in their places, and after more experience with Indian children, will probably succeed. But few of the pupils are very far advanced. Of the more advanced pupils now in the school, most of them are not beyond division in arithmetic, though a few are in fractions; and some of them are studying 'Cornell's Intermediate Geography.'

"It is an interesting fact that the industries are exceptionally prominent at this school. All the buildings, save the one first erected, were made by the boys, aided by the carpenters. They are nearly all of adobe, but much better than the common Mexican adobe buildings, well ceiled, with roofing of lumber, and abounding in conveniences, such as we are accustomed to find in our older communities. Seven boys work regularly for one-half day in the carpenter's shop, others mend shoes, others do turning, painting, glazing, pipe-laying, and general repairing. About thirty boys work on the farm from three to four and a half hours each day; others cut wood.

"The school farm consists of forty-two acres, every

rod of which is excellent soil, well irrigated. A good variety of vegetables is raised for the school, and eighty tons of wheat and barley and barley-hay were raised last year, which brings in the market at this place twelve dollars per ton.

"Last year Mr. Billman hired one hundred acres of land for the purpose of teaching the adult Papagoes lessons in farming, as well as to help them in self-support. He brought in ten Papago families from the desert, and put them into small temporary houses near the leased lands, to cultivate them. Agent Crouse gave some ploughs, and Mr. Billman bought the seed and some harness, which latter he loaned to the Indians. These people brought their ponies for ploughing, etc. The schoolboys and farmers were sent into the fields to work with and show the Indians. To illustrate how the work should be done, a heavy team with a large plough was set at work, and the smaller Indian teams were kept at work at the same time. In the early part of the season, while the Indians were ploughing, sowing, etc., Mr. Billman supplied them with subsistence, keeping an account of the same. In due time the grain was cut and baled, and Mr. Billman marketed the grain, allowing the Indians half the hay. After paying for their living during the season, each head of the family had from thirty to seventy dollars left. The care of this experiment, in addition to all his other labors, was too exacting for Mr. Billman, and his health seriously suffered, on account of which he has been unable to repeat the experiment this year.

"There is an excellent hospital, but the school has few patients — none on the occasion of my visit — and there is only about one death each year."

Mrs. Dorchester makes an additional report, giving discriminating details of the girls' departments, which are of equal interest. With such schools and teachers, the Indian problem will gradually be solved.

## VIII

## THROUGH THE DESERT TO PARADISE

CACTI — THE COLORADO RIVER — YUMA AND THE INDIANS — BELOW THE OCEAN — A CALIFORNIA RIDDLE

THE territory of Arizona is the southwestern corner of the United States. Its western boundary is the Colorado River, which flows with a large volume of water through Yuma to the Gulf of California, and is one of the great rivers of America. The day had been hot and dusty, and our journey, though novel and interesting at first, was becoming monotonous. A small amount of desert is satisfying, and our specimen had been very large. As the train wound among dreary sand-hills, only to emerge upon drearier plains dotted with huge cacti, thorn-bushes, sage-brush, and mesquit trees, the heat became intense, and we were indeed thankful that there was no wind to raise sand-clouds, since even the motion of the train enveloped the rear cars in whirls of fine dust. Far away to the west were purple hills, and around us mirage-haunted plains.

On these plains and hills grow all kinds of cacti. There are, in the three states of California, Arizona, and New Mexico, more than one hundred species of cacti, eight of yucca, and seven of agave. Among these, the most wonderful is the giant cactus, whose green fluted columns, with grotesque arms and thorny ridges, may be seen upon the high plains and hills of the Arizona and California deserts. They are huge, misshapen growths, deformities of nature, without a single redeeming feature, yet they are not without use to man. Though growing in a dry and thirsty land, where no water is, they secrete a liquid which is a fair substitute for the precious treasure, and their thorns contain a resin of which the Indians make torches. At this season (the early spring) a beautiful pear-shaped and cream-colored flower grows out among the thorny spikes, and later on fruit ripens. This is edible for men, and is chiefly eaten by birds. The "yuccas" are seen from San Antonio to the Pacific. They are variously named, the "Roman candle," the "Spanish bayonet," the "Whipplei," and the "dagger plant" being some of the names given to this ornamental and magnificent production. It grows on the dry and sandy soil, and often seems to spring directly from a rock. Its leaves are green reeds, sharp and thin, from two to three feet long, and they spread out in every direction around the stalk. This grows to the height of twelve or fifteen feet, and is as large as a small tree at the base and grows to a point. At about half its height from the ground, little twigs begin to put out, and upon these are hung with divine art multitudes of little bell-shaped flowers. There are sometimes more than a thousand of these delicate bells upon a single stem. In color, shape, and odor, the flower resembles the tuberose, and the effect of these lovely white yuccas, rising on their tall and tapering stalk, from warlike nests of dagger-leaves, by hundreds on the desert hills and plains, is weird and beautiful by day or in the evening.

The *agave*, or American aloe, is known to us as the "century plant," but in warm climates there is no foundation for such a name. Its roots and leaves furnish, by distillation, a variety of strong liquors; its thorns are needles and pins, and its fibre is good for firewood or paper-making. The Mexicans make a popular drink called *pulque* by scooping out the bud and leaving a natural bowl for the sap to flow into. This liquid, which flows to the amount of a gallon or more daily, is placed in vats and fermented. Thus, instead of nourishing the beautiful flower which blooms but for a brief season, the life-blood of the plant intoxicates and stupefies Mexican drunkards. To such base uses are God's choicest gifts applied!

All sorts of cacti grow in profusion on these plains and mountains. Sometimes the plain is covered with their ugly bristles and thorns, among which multitudes of yellow and scarlet and crimson and red flowers are sprinkled — beautiful gems of color protected by ten thousand poisoned spears. Every part of the earth is full of the wonderful works of the Creator, and even the barren desert declares in mighty and awful tones his great name.

From the midst of the Arizona desert we came direct to Yuma, and then went down into the California desert. But Yuma is a wonderful place, for here the Colorado River, after its junction with the Gila, comes pouring an immense flood towards the

Gulf of California. The San Jacinto range of mountains rises, six miles distant, to the height of ten thousand feet, full of wild and rocky ravines, and its serrated sides bear testimony to the floods which pour down to swell the Colorado in the rainy season. Vegetation watered by this great river is rich and abundant here. The climate is reported as without fault. The clear, bracing air of the timbered mountains tempers the air of the valley, the mighty river cools and freshens it, the cañon of giant palms and tropical verdure is close at hand, and the breezes of the gulf, dried by their passage over the desert, give refreshment without dampness.

The Colorado River rises in the territory of Wyoming, on the western slope of the Rocky Mountains. It gathers the streams of Wyoming, Colorado, Utah, New Mexico, and Arizona. It flows across arid table-lands, and through porous soils which evaporate and absorb its waters, but it nevertheless is a large and impressive stream as it sweeps past Yuma to find its outlet in the Gulf of California. Plans have been formed to make Yuma a great town, with water, and light, and electric cars, and a huge hotel. The surrounding country can be made fertile by irrigation. Oranges, lemons, figs, dates, grapes, and pomegranates will all grow here, and ripen a month earlier than in Southern California. The Yuma Indians are peaceable, but unprogressive and indolent. They hold a large territory of fine, unimproved land along the Colorado, which will doubtless become the property of white settlers by easy purchase, for a kind of paralysis seems to rest upon these Indian tribes which prevents them from using the opportunities for advancement which the United States government now offers to them. Compulsory civilization and education do not suit the Indian nature, and the result of the settlement of this continent by white men has been disastrous to the aborigines. They have been abused, and robbed, and destroyed in the name of civilization and Christianity, though they were not a weak, an unintelligent, or an ignorant race. Their own acts have hastened their decline, but the chief responsibility for their fate rests upon the government of the United States, or, to put it more plainly and personally, upon the American people who have taken their lands, their game, and their lives. Some tardy amends are being attempted among certain tribes, but the waves of Anglo-Saxon civilization will in another generation engulf and sweep away all remnants of aboriginal nationality.

From Yuma we descend into what was once the bed of the sea. Great heaps of sea sand shine in the sunlight, and are swept by the winds hither and thither. There seems little reason to doubt that the ocean was once here, for there are great bodies of salt now profitably mined near Salton, on the Southern Pacific Railroad. From Cactus, near Yuma, which is three hundred and ninety-five feet above the sea, the road descends till it is two hundred and sixty-three feet below the sea. A place called Flowing Wells is five feet above the sea, then the traveller comes to the margin of an inland sea, or an ocean beach, and for sixty miles travels much farther below the ocean-level than at any point in the low countries of Europe. It is thought that parts of this salt desert may be reclaimed by irrigation, but no attempts have been made upon a sufficiently extensive scale to test the matter.

We went to sleep in the dry desert; when we woke, a hard rain was pelting upon the roof of the car, and on looking out of the window, a scene of green and gold, washed by a downpour worthy of the Atlantic coast, burst upon our astonished vision. We were in California, in the midst of the wonderful orange groves of Riverside, which have no equal in the world. Piles of oranges lay on the ground as far as the eye could see through the vistas of the orchards. The trees were laden with the golden fruit. Huge eucalyptus trees in full and fragrant flower, palms of all sorts, vegetation rank and rich and green, and all the more impressive from the desert dream from which we woke to this wonderful reality, was all about us. This is California, the land of gold, the paradise of climates, the home of health, the retreat for the aged who would live forever, and for the invalid who dreads to die. And it is raining as if another flood were coming, and is cold enough to chill a salamander. Let us investigate. I put on goloshes and a heavy mackintosh, and with a big umbrella launched into the deep mud of my first California town. It grew wetter and wetter, muddier and muddier, and more beautiful every step that I advanced. I walked an hour amid scenes of tropical loveliness, flowers, trees, fruits; and came back to the car as wet and cold as if I had been at Coney Island in a March northeaster.

# IX

## IN CALIFORNIA

CLIMATE AND WEATHER — VARIED PRODUCTIONS — INHABITANTS — RIVERSIDE AND ITS ORANGES — HORTICULTURE AND ITS RESULTS

IN order to write truthfully and intelligently of California, special regard must be had to its varying climate and unique situation. There is a rainy season and a dry season; daytime, when the sun is hot, and there is little wind from sunrise to ten or eleven o'clock; afternoon, when the wind comes up and blows till near sundown; then the night comes, usually still, and always cold. The only feature of weather that can be always relied upon, so far as I have been able to ascertain, is the cool nights. The day may be warm, windy, variable, or unchanged in temperature and quality; the night will always be cold. It may be dry enough to sleep in the open air, but it will be cold enough to require several blankets. Such curious conditions of climate, where winter is warmer than summer, and where dense clouds do not imply that rain is coming, where the cold of the night more than averages the heat of day, where some vegetation grows continuously the year through, and other sorts pass through a period of

CALIFORNIA ROSE GARDEN

growth, decline, and rest, entirely confuse the steady-going observer on the Atlantic coast, who is accustomed to the four seasons,— spring, summer, autumn, and winter. A resident of Santa Barbara remarked to me, that "the usual variation of temperature between midnight and noon was greater than between winter and summer"; another one said, "When I go out to make a call on a July afternoon, I always wear my heavy overcoat." A friend who has been here for a year told me that he was obliged to go in his shirt-sleeves for comfort in December and January during the day, and that a fur wrap was not uncomfortable when riding in the evening.

It is evident from such statements that California has a climate of its own, and cannot properly be described as the Italy of America, nor its coast compared in its climatic conditions with the Riviera, with Malaga and Southern Spain, or with Sicily. It is a country by itself, lying between the vast watery mass of the Pacific Ocean and lofty ranges of mountains, whose summits are snow-clad for a large portion of the year. This comparatively narrow region, which forms the state, has every variety of altitude, from the moors which skirt the seacoast, to the lovely little table-lands hidden far up in the cañons among the mountains. It has rolling hills and broad levels, forests of liveoaks and sycamores, and plains devoted to orchards and vineyards, to barley fields and gardens. It has rivers like those of Sicily and Spain, with dry beds, except when rain-storms come, which then become rushing torrents with an immense volume of water that overflow land and sweep everything before them in their resistless course. It has winds from the Pacific Ocean and from the snow-clad peaks which divide the continent, and one can no more predict when they will blow, nor how long they will continue, than Nicodemus could tell whence the wind cometh and whither it goeth. It has not the climate, the characteristics, nor the soil of any other country as a specialty, but it is peculiar and unique in all these respects. But one can find in different parts of this large state, resemblances to many different regions, and the productions of nearly all. Wheat as fine as that of Minnesota grows here, and figs as delicious as those of the south of France. Asparagus and artichokes, oysters and shad, apples, peaches, and oranges, potatoes and pomegranates, beans and bananas, are natives in California. There is no better beef and mutton in the world, and California horses, mules, and asses are unsurpassed. Every kind of wood, from the easily worked redwood to the tough live-oak, grows in the state, though a large portion of its area is destitute of trees, and building materials of stone and brick are abundant.

The state has a heterogeneous population composed of a large proportion of Americans, children of early settlers, and emigrants from the East, mingled with Indians, Mexicans, and Chinese; and colonies of Danes, Spaniards, Portuguese, and Canadians, who often live in isolated communities, continuing their own customs, language, and religious habits and associations. It is not possible for a traveller to judge how far such conditions have influenced the growth and development of the state, but he can understand the influences which have been most potent in certain towns and districts, and the advantages which have accrued to some sections on account of the character of its settlement.

Our entrance to the state was at the town of Riverside, and though the day was cold, and the rain fell in torrents, it was impossible not to recognize the region as one of the most rich and abundant orange-growing parts of the state. The crop was ripening fast, and heaps of the golden fruit lay in the orchards, while the trees seemed still to have heavier loads than the branches could sustain. The fruit grown here commands a high price, and is of fine size and quality.

I shall never forget the time when, coming from the African desert by way of El Arish, the caravan reached Jaffa on the Mediterranean Sea, and wound through narrow streets lined with huge baskets piled high with large and luscious oranges. But even the memories of that scene fade and pale before the golden view of the Riverside orchards. When the rain ceased and the sun shone out, the scene was bewilderingly gorgeous. We became gradually accustomed to orange orchards, to enormous piles of fruit, to Chinamen gathering and washing and sorting and packing oranges by hundreds of thousands, but the first views of the orange garden of Riverside will always remain as the type and standard of orange culture and its attractions in Southern California.

Great companies, like the Earle Fruit Company, purchase, pack, and ship the fruit in special cars which hold three hundred boxes. They have packing-houses along the railway to which the fruit is brought. It is received and placed on large slanting platforms, and by ingenious contrivances the different sizes sort themselves. Chinamen rapidly seize, and wrap, and place these in prepared boxes, other Chinamen, using a simple machine, press down and nail on the covers, and stack them for packing in the refrigerator cars. During the busy season the work often goes on far into the night, as well as all day. In 1891, the crop of Southern California was about five thousand carloads, or a million and a half boxes of oranges. In 1893, it was much larger, for many trees had come into bearing during the interval. Oranges, like all good things in this world, need cultivation; and they repay care and culture. Great care must be used in the selection and growth of the trees. The orchards must be ploughed and kept clear of weeds, water must be abundantly and judiciously provided during the long dry seasons, the trees must be guarded from insects, and the limbs supported as the fruit matures; all the fruit must be hand-picked, cleaned, and dried, fairly sized, well wrapped, and boxed.

The best fruit, the Washington navel orange grown at Riverside, is a large, seedless orange of a high color, skin of medium thickness, delicious flavor, and much juice. It surpasses any fruit grown in the Florida orchards, and is, to my taste, the best orange in the world. The finest of this sort command, even here, from two to three dollars a box.

One never wearies of walking through the groves

and driving along Magnolia Avenue, and seeing and hearing of this delightful branch of horticulture in the fragrant air and the warm sun of Southern California. All is not gold that glitters, and golden oranges do not always turn to gold in the pockets of the fruit raisers, but the industry is a pleasant and profitable one, and those who enter upon it with sufficient capital, and pursue it with perseverance and enterprise, are pretty sure of success.

Lemons are more difficult to raise than oranges, the tree being more delicate and susceptible to frost. If the lemons are picked before they are ripe, and carefully cured, the skin grows thin, and the juice increases greatly, and after a few months their value is doubled or trebled. Lemons thus treated have brought six dollars a box, and the market is never overstocked. San Bernardino County, in which Riverside is located, has nearly half of the lemon trees of the state.

The raisin business has also an important centre at Riverside, and the California raisins have now taken the place in the United States of the imported raisin to a large extent. A vineyard of raisin grapes begins to yield by the third year, and by the fifth year has reached its full yield of two hundred boxes to the acre. This product has increased in California from six thousand boxes to more than three million boxes in twenty years, and it is still increasing. Even as far north as Fresno, Noble Brothers and the Fresno Home Packing Company do a large and valuable business in this fruit. I have only touched upon those fruits which make Riverside a profitable as well as a beautiful place. The broad streets bordered with palm trees, and shaded with tall, swinging branches of eucalyptus trees; with miles of homes in the midst of orange groves, and an intelligent, happy, and prosperous population; with good schools, well supplied churches, and agreeable society, make this a favorite town for visitors and residents. We were sorry to leave it, but the time had come to move on, and we took the train for San Diego.

# X

## CORONADO BEACH

A NARROW ESCAPE — FINE WEATHER — A LUXURY TO LIVE — ACRES OF WILD FLOWERS — BEAUTY ON SEA AND SHORE — COMFORT AND GOOD COMPANY — EXCURSIONS — BLUE PRESBYTERIANISM

IT was well that we did not linger longer in Riverside, for the floods were out and travelling was dangerous. Two hours after our heavy Pullman train passed over the Southern California road from Riverside to San Diego, bridges and embankments gave way under the pressure of the waters, and nearly a week elapsed before the damages were repaired. We were thankful that we had escaped from disaster, and were housed in such a delightful place as the Hotel del Coronado, across the harbor from San Diego, on the shores of the Pacific, at Coronado Beach. For a day or two after our arrival there was rain and fog, and we began to think that the climate of Southern California was beautiful only in books. Then the sun came out bright, and though mists partially shrouded the distant mountains and lay far out upon the ocean, there was no more rain, and the weather prophets declared that the "rainy season" was over. There certainly seemed to be water enough everywhere. It was impossible to make any excursions to the Mission, to Tia Juana, or to Point Loma, for bridges had gone away, and fords had changed their bottom, and the roads were gullied and washed beyond repair. But there was no need for excursions in order to enjoyment. It was a luxury to sit, on a March morning, with the shade of a palm tree over one's head, and the warm sun upon one's feet, and the cool breeze bringing the ozone of the Pacific Ocean to the lungs, and to gaze over the beautiful blue of the sea or follow the exquisite curve of the shore, which has not inaptly been compared to the famous Bay of Naples. After long railway journeys through deserts and over mountains, sleeping and eating in narrow quarters, and at the rate of thirty miles an hour, we could appreciate the spacious rooms, the manifold comforts, the varied and excellent fare, the rest, recreation, and refreshment of a first-class hotel. We were conscious, too, of a new atmosphere, soft and balmy, and yet pure and strengthening. For a few days after the rain, there was a chill in the air which suggested snow, like the wind that blows from the north in early spring; but after a little this was modified, and day after day the thermometer marked sixty degrees, as if it were fixed at that point, the sun came out clear and bright, the wind blew steadily from the same point, and Nature moved gradually forward all her beautiful creations of tree and shrub and plant in a wonderful procession. The fields were literally carpeted with wild flowers : yellow daisies and poppies in masses so dense that the hills seemed vast

RAMONA'S MARRIAGE PLACE, SAN DIEGO

heaps of gold, valleys so filled with the flowers of the wild onion that one seemed to look upon a great deposit of sapphires, the glowing red of the "painter's brush" in a flaming line through greens so rich and bright that their reproduction on canvas would be pronounced an exaggeration. Wherever the eye wandered there was beauty, from the aquamarine of the sea, edged along the shore with a ruffled foam crest of breakers, and higher up with a band of yellow sand, to the flowery hills and meadows, the dark mountains covered with the close foliage of the liveoaks, the distant peaks glistening in their crowns of snow, and over all a firmament of pure and ethereal blue in which the sun blazed bright all day long, and the moon and stars shone like radiant jewels by night. The beach, twelve miles long, with its never wearying play of waves; or the smooth waters of the Bay of San Diego, forming the foreground for a picturesque view of the town built on hills, with the mountains still further back; or Point Loma, a huge headland, at whose base stands the lighthouse that is now used, and on whose summit rises the lighthouse which has now been abandoned; and the wild mountains down towards the Mexican border, offer to the resident at Coronado Beach every variety of scenery, while drives and excursions along the shores, or inland to the valleys, furnish abundant means of recreation. The botanist may here fill his herbarium with new varieties of plants daily, and with seaweeds rich and rare; there are shells in great variety and beauty upon the beaches for the conchologist to gather and arrange, there are fish that are worth catching, and no end of small game — hares, and ducks, and quail — to be found within a short ride of Coronado. A party which went from the hotel during my visit had five days of capital sport, and brought home a bag of more than seven hundred game. Such hunts are frequent, and the table is never without all kinds of game that are in season.

Coronado Beach is twelve miles long, expanding into a plain at its northern end, which is opposite San Diego. Upon the south front of the beach, and close to the sea, the hotel has been built. It is a building that covers four and one-half acres of ground, and is a surprising combination of Spanish and American ideas. The manifold angles and curves of its many fronts, its bays and piazzas, bewilder the eye, and one is at a loss to say whether it belongs to any style of architecture. Within is a large hall, which opens into an interior court like the Spanish *patio*. This is laid out in paved walks, with flower beds, in the midst of which are royal and date palms, India-rubber trees, flowering shrubs, and climbing vines. The house is full of flowers. Every public room has its vases of roses, and lilies, and hyacinths, and every table in the vast dining-room has for its central ornament an exquisite bouquet. Provision is made here for all sorts of people, for differing tastes, and various degrees of physical strength. Glass piazzas give an enclosed walk of a quarter of a mile without turning; great tanks of salt and fresh water invite those who desire to swim without the risk of the surf to their pure depths; delightful gardens with exquisitely framed beds of flowers and plants, and shady retreats, offer a lounging place to the weary or feeble. Well-chosen walks, an ostrich farm, a bewildering maze, bowling-alleys, and all the indoor amusements which a well-appointed watering place affords are here.

But the charm of the place is out of doors, under the palm trees, by the seashore, on a horse or in a carriage. Riding over the hills, into the cañons, breathing such air as our lungs in New York never receive, rejoicing in the fact of existence, and feeling no unpleasant reproach of conscience for doing nothing except enjoy the works and ways of God, we pass our days, and have quite forgotten that there is such a thing as news, or a condition of life where a newspaper is a daily necessity. Such a place is Coronado Beach, and those who go there pass their time in such varied and delightful occupations.

One day, in choice company with an enthusiastic artist and amateur photographers, we drove around the coast to the headland which forms the entrance of the land-locked harbor of San Diego. Sitting on the hill-side, we could watch the *Santa Rosa*, one of the largest steamers on the Pacific coast, as she made her way through the channel near the shore for four or five miles out to sea, and then doubled on her track, rounded Point Loma and steamed northwards on her voyage to San Francisco. Before us lay the harbor and its shipping, and beyond the picturesque town on sloping hill-sides; at the right the long curve of the beach swept down to the Mexican border; and behind all, the outline of mountains was dimly seen, through a haze like that which sometimes veils our

New England heights in the August days. The artist's ready pencil seized the outlines and brilliant colors of the scene, which will grow under his deft fingers into a lovely painting, while many a sun picture was taken by the cameras which will increase the pleasures of memory in days to come.

Another afternoon found us visiting the old town of San Diego, where the first wooden house in California still stands. Its timbers were framed in New England, and carried around Cape Horn to be erected here. Not far distant was the residence of a companion of Richard H. Dana, in his "Two Years Before the Mast." He married and settled in San Diego, and has only recently died, leaving a large number of descendants, who are of a lighter color than most of the people among whom they live. There, too, is the church in which "Ramona," the heroine of Helen Hunt Jackson's novel, was married, and some of the descriptions of scenery and customs in that well-written and philanthropic book, had their originals in this place. The old town is almost abandoned, for speculation, which has done much good and also much evil in California, invaded San Diego not many years since. Land was laid out in lots, from the highlands to low-water mark, and was sold and resold until the "boom" burst. Then a new town had arisen, hundreds of people had been ruined, and many Eastern people had invested their money in lots over whose rotting stakes the tide now rises and falls daily. All over California there have been similar experiences of speculation. There is still much good land to be had in the world at reasonable rates, and fortunes will not be lost anywhere by judicious waiting.

We drove one day to the old Mission, whose adobe walls are tumbling down, while near at hand is a large Roman Catholic "contract" school, full of Indian boys and girls. The priest had tried that morning to cross the river in a wagon, but his horse lost footing in the quicksands, kicked himself loose, swam ashore, and left the "padre" sitting in the vehicle in the middle of the river. From this ludicrous and somewhat dangerous position, he had just been rescued by his pupils when we came upon the scene. The old Franciscans made good selections for their foundations, and builded better than they knew in some cases. But most of their buildings are now in ruins, and their day in California has long been ended. Half a century ago, none but Roman Catholics could reside in California, and many English and Americans joined the Roman Church in order to trade in the country. Now there is freedom for every faith, and I attended service in a Presbyterian church at Coronado, built as a memorial, and heard as thorough a Calvinistic sermon as ever was preached in Geneva or Edinburgh. Some called the preacher "narrow," while others were pleased that he was "true blue," and I was glad that I could worship God in this far country after the custom of my ancestors.

## XI

## PASADENA

SIGNING TICKETS — BREAKING A TRAIN IN TWO — OCEAN VIEWS — MEETING DR. ORMISTON — HIS GOOD WORK — FRIENDS IN PASADENA — A BIG ROSE-BUSH — THE CROWN OF THE VALLEY — A MODEL TOWN

If we were to see California, we must leave Coronado Beach and begin our journey, for the state is large, there are many beautiful and interesting places to visit, and we were tourists and not home-seekers. So we checked our trunks, paying a dollar each in addition to our railway fares, to have them taken from the hotel at the beach to the hotel at Pasadena. In these new states, where the journeys are long and hard, the railway companies are very strict, and careful not to do any extra work without getting pay for it. Railway officials and magnates, and their friends, are treated munificently, but the ordinary traveller pays his way at a high price for all that he receives. The ferry-boat took us across the harbor to San Diego, and we were at the station in good time. It was well that we were, for there was a great crowd, and the line to the ticket-office was long and, for the most part, patient. There was one angry man. He had waited for his turn to come, and had his own and a friend's ticket in his hand. For some reason not explained to me, but evidently familiar to the crowd, each purchaser of a ticket was obliged to sign his name on the ticket. Men, women, and children had been handed a pen as they paid their fares or showed their tickets, and each had inscribed his name, which was a sort of tribute to the widespread education of California. When this man's turn came, he objected to signing. The ticket seller insisted that it was necessary, and the man expostulated. Finally he signed, and then wanted to sign the other ticket for his friend, who was lame. This could not be allowed. In a rage he exclaimed: "I have travelled all over Europe, and never had to sign a ticket." "Wall, you've got to sign it here," drawled the official, adding, in the most insulting manner: "See here, gents, is a feller who's travelled all over Urup!" The man saw that the sympathy of the crowd was with the ticket seller, and so marched off and hurried his lame comrade into the line, where he stood for half an hour before his turn came to sign.

Before this tedious operation was completed, the train drew up. There was one specially coveted "chair car," a clumsy contrivance for reducing the misery of a railway ride. Having received early information of this extra comfort, which could not be secured beforehand, though it had to be paid for afterwards, I covenanted with a powerful San Diegan to secure seats for us, which he did by dexterously pitching our bags through the open windows as the car slid by, leaping himself on the rear platform, and installing the luggage before the scramble began. We followed at our ease, and found our Hercules, who surrendered his fortifications, received his bribe, and retired to win other similar victories. The day was hot, and the train was crowded with people standing in the aisles, except in the "chair car," for an excursion of an independent order of Elks or Buffaloes, or some such society, was going to the Capistrano Mission or to Oceanside for a picnic. The load was so heavy that, in going up a hill near one of the recent washouts, the train broke in two, and a good many of the Elks were landed at the bottom of the hill in some confusion, but without any broken bones.

As we rode along, the landscape charmed and delighted the eye. On one side was the Pacific Ocean, the shore fringed with small islands and foam-whitened reefs; on the other side were hills and valleys covered with flowers, yellow poppies, blue and yellow and white violets, daisies, and baby-blue-eyes. Orange orchards and fields of barley of a bright and brilliant green succeeded; then groves of liveoak; and beyond, the purple and black mountain sides with their crowns of snow, which generally remain till the middle of May. The ride was through fine scenery, but the sun was hot.

A little after noon we reached Los Angeles, where there was a change, and a hurried scramble for the next train, as our train was late, and on taking our seats, we found directly in front of us the Rev. Dr. William Ormiston, the former pastor of the Collegiate Reformed Church at Twenty-ninth Street, New

PASADENA AND MOUNT WILSON

York. "And where have you dropped from, and how do you do, my dear friends!" was his hearty greeting. We had a pleasant talk then, and afterwards I visited him at his ranch at Azusa, and wandered with him in his orange groves, which embrace in all about one hundred acres, and sat with him in his study till the evening shadows fell, purpling the mountains, and then bore with me to my temporary home a quantity of golden fruit, which kept the lunch-basket full for several days. Dr. Ormiston is the same warm-hearted, earnest man whom so many of my readers have known, and he told me that no Sunday passed that he did not break the bread of life to some congregation, rarely in the large towns, usually in some mountain glen, or on a ranch distant from any church. Several of these little congregations have become organized churches, and have pastors or preachers of their own. Much work of this sort can be done and is done in California, and it will bear spiritual fruit among these orchards and vineyards in days to come.

When I was settled comfortably in the town of Pasadena, I found that it was the residence or stopping place of many friends. Here was the Rev. Robert Strong, whose work in the systematic benevolence of their church has made him known to so many Presbyterians. Here dwells also, not beneath his own vine and fig tree, but beneath a climbing "Gold of Ophir" rose-bush which in one year had more than fifty thousand blossoms, the Rev. A. M. Merwin, some time missionary of the Presbyterian Board in South America, and now superintendent of the Board's work among the Mexicans of Southern California. Palms and orange trees surround the house, and its outlook is enchanting.

Pasadena, "the crown of the valley," was founded just twenty years ago, by an association of gentlemen from Indianapolis, in the northwest corner of the San Gabriel Valley at the base of the Sierra Madre Mountains. They intended only to raise oranges and lemons, and they have builded a city which now has a population of from ten to twelve thousand. The city is built on high, rolling land, sloping southward from the Sierra Madre Mountains towards the sea, which is twenty-five miles distant, and on the eastern bank of a clear mountain stream which supplies all the water needed for irrigation or for domestic uses. Mountains, only five miles distant, rise in the north to a height of six thousand feet above the valley, enclosing, with lesser peaks, the great undulating plain of the San Gabriel River, which stretches eastward for sixty miles.

Pasadena commands this prospect, and from some of its heights offers glimpses of the Pacific. The town is laid out in broad avenues and streets, mostly rectangular, but some curving, notably the beautiful Orange Grove Avenue. These are well paved, and lined with many varieties of semi-tropical shade trees, among which palms and eucalyptus are prominent. The houses stand in orchards and gardens, with a profusion of beautiful and fragrant flowers, which are to be seen nowhere except in Southern California. Some of the residences are costly villas of elegant architectural design, like those of Professor Lowe and Governor Markham, but the majority of houses in Pasadena are homes where culture and refinement have their abiding place, in company with contentment and happiness.

The character of the citizens of this town makes it an eminently desirable place to live. The town has not grown up hap-hazard, made up of drift-wood and débris, but it was founded by intelligent Christian people, and this kind of people have added to its population, and live there to-day. The people all go to church on the Sabbath, and one-fourth of the residents are church-members; they are absolutely destitute of a saloon or grog-shop; they have one of the best public libraries in the state; they take pride in having well-paved, well-cleaned, well-watered, and well-lighted streets; they have six first-class schoolhouses, with nine rooms in each, and out of the ten thousand inhabitants fifteen hundred are enrolled as scholars. About two thousand Eastern people annually test the climate and pleasures of Pasadena, and a proportion of these always become permanent residents. The people are engaged in fruit growing, trade, manufactures, banking, and too many of them in real estate transactions. But as the land is sold, and this city of twenty years of age settles into a substantial and steadily growing town, the mania for land speculation, which is developed in all young communities, will give place to better employments. Thus far, Pasadena has more than realized the expectations of its founders, and there are few places in Southern California where better climate, and water, and soil, and society, and civil and religious privileges are combined.

## XII

## IN THE SAN GABRIEL VALLEY

EXCURSIONS IN THE VALLEY — LUCKY BALDWIN AND HIS RANCH — SUNNY SLOPE VINEYARDS — THE OLD MISSION — A MOUNTAIN RAILROAD — EASTER SUNDAY AT PASADENA.

PASADENA is the centre from which pleasant drives and mountain excursions and visits to ranches and orchards radiate. Our days were not too many for the plans which were made to fill them with pleasure. The mornings often dawned with fog lying over the landscape, as we see it in the river valleys of New England in summer time. Such mornings are troublesome to invalids, for the fog comes from the Pacific Ocean, and is hurtful to the lungs of the consumptive, and irritating to the asthmatic. Before noon it is all gone, and the atmosphere is dry, and the sun warm. On a bright morning we took our places with an agreeable party that just filled the three seats of a fine buckboard built in Maine. The accomplished driver sat in solitary solemnity upon a single high-perched seat in front, from which he handled the reins and flourished the whip with great dexterity over the backs of four well-groomed bays that formed our team. They were all sleek, handsome horses, fat as almost all the California horses are, because of the excellence of their food, but fleet of foot and showing excellent endurance at a good pace for hours. Over roads that become hard and smooth as soon as the rains cease, between avenues of the rapidly growing eucalyptus trees, which have been planted throughout California, in the fresh, delicious air full of perfume from thousands of flowers, we spun along in the San Gabriel valley. This valley has an area of about three hundred and fifty thousand acres of arable land, which is irrigated and sometimes devastated by the San Gabriel River. The Sierra Madre Mountains rise on the north from six to seven thousand feet above the sea-level, and there are hills upon the other sides which shut out violent winds. These favored lands are occupied by the fruitful ranches of many prosperous farmers, and among them are attractive resorts, comfortable hotels, and mountain camps, occupied by health and pleasure seekers from all parts of the world. The frostless valley, with orange groves and fine homes, at the foot of mountains covered with snow in the winter and spring months, and the Pacific Ocean in view from the foot-hills about twenty miles away, is an ideal place in which to live.

Among these residents is "Lucky Baldwin," whose ranch is one of the show-places. This sobriquet indicates his good fortune. In the garden near his fine house stands the original one-man cabin which he built many years ago, when he came to try his luck in California. He now has fifty thousand acres of the best land in the heart of the San Gabriel valley, the best stock farm in Southern California, three large and thriving hotels, one of which is in San Francisco, and wealth of all kinds. Such are the possibilities in many parts of our great, fertile, and growing country. Sagacity, industry, strength, and perseverance are sure to gain success in connection with these great opportunities. The men who fail would fail anywhere, but the men who succeed would not by any means be successful in our older and more conservative communities. There are difficulties to be overcome, and there is hard work to be done, and judgment is to be exercised in California and Oregon and Washington, as well as in Eastern places, but the road to success is shorter and easier here.

"Lucky Baldwin" has fine flowing wells of pure water, groves of planted trees, orange orchards that yield him fifteen hundred dollars an acre each year, cattle that take the prizes in Southern California, and beautiful horses that have made a name east of the Rocky Mountains. He gets his water from Artesian wells, valley and mountain streams, and from large storage reservoirs, dams, and pipe systems, having in operation many miles of irrigation pipes of large size, and a complete system of reservoirs and pressure pipes for domestic use.

Oranges are his chief crop, but apples and cherries and plums and grapes, grain, vegetables, and nuts, swell the list of his agricultural products, and his horses are many and beautiful. We visited the stalls and admired the fine animals as the proud grooms removed their blankets, and expatiated upon their pedigree and points. Some were playful as kittens, while others were as sensitive as a high-born maiden. All were cared for with vigilant attention, regularly exercised, judiciously clothed and fed, and treated as animals should be who are worth thousands in their own right, and other thousands which they could earn for their fortunate owner.

From this ranch we drove to the "sunny slope" vineyards, through acres of stumpy vines which were just beginning to shoot, to the storage cellars, where rows of huge casks and shelves of bottles full of choice wine are kept. Men were busy putting up orders for the Eastern market, and samples of the various productions were at hand for buyers or tasters. The wine of California has a strong fruity taste, which is not acceptable to those who have been long accustomed to the manufactured wines which come across the sea. I have no experience in the sample-room, and can only wonder at the cultivation of the sense of taste which enables an expert to believe the story of two tasters at Heidelberg who disagreed about the contents of a huge tun of wine. One tasted leather, and another tasted iron. When the wine was drawn off, a rusty key with a leather tag was found at the bottom of the great cask, and the reputation of both of the tasters was established. The California wine, as it comes from these ranches, is pure and true juice of the grape, though I am told that great quantities are sold which are afterwards doctored to suit cultivated palates, and labelled with the brands of popular French vineyards.

In one of the yards of this ranch a lot of Chinamen

were washing and brushing and sorting oranges, chattering and laughing as they worked, under the direction of an American inspector. They worked rapidly and thoroughly, and the trays of fruit, as the sun dried it, were carried off to the packing-house, and thence in wagon-loads of boxes to the railway.

One of our drives took in the San Gabriel Mission, with its ancient chime of bells, wonderful grapevine, and Mexican inhabitants. The contrast between this sleepy Spanish village, with its rows of wine-shops, adobe houses, and ancient air, with brisk and thrifty Pasadena — prohibition, enterprising, Protestant — was amazing. While we were at Pasadena, Professor Lowe gave, one evening, a lecture, with fine photographic views to illustrate a new attraction in the neighborhood. This is an engineering enterprise whose object is to connect Los Angeles and Pasadena with Wilson's Peak and the summit of the San Gabriel range of mountains, upward of six thousand feet above the sea. The road is completed from Altadena along the higher foot-hills and up through Rubio Cañon, a distance of two or three miles, and thence by a steep cable incline to the summit of Echo Mountain, thirty-five hundred feet above the Pacific. Here a large hotel, capable of accommodating several hundred guests, is being built. The place has already been occupied by invalids who are greatly benefited by the tonic air, and who have camped in the neighborhood for a number of years. The hotel occupies a commanding position. From its verandas a wonderful view of mountains, cultivated valleys, towns, and villages, orange groves, villa residences, and distant ocean greets the vision. About twenty miles of bridle roads have been constructed from the Echo Mountain House to neighboring summits, cañons, cascades, picturesque rocks, wooded ravines, ferny dells, and other points of interest; and there will be no lack of attraction for the tourist who is lifted to Echo Mountain summit on the great cable incline. From the latter point the railroad will be extended by easy grades along the ridge overlooking Grand Cañon and through several mountain valleys to the summit of Mount Lowe, the highest point visible from Pasadena, where the great Summit Hotel will command a horizon more than one hundred miles distant in every direction.

Immediately north of Mount Lowe is the highest point in the range, known as Observatory Peak, 6723 feet above the sea, or about four hundred feet higher than Mount Washington. It is reserved for the site of a great observatory, and correspondence is pending which, it is hoped, will secure for it the construction of the largest telescope in the world.

We were at Pasadena on Easter Sunday. On Saturday it seemed as if the flowers of a kingdom had come into the town, so fragrant was the air and so occupied with flowers were the people. Sunday dawned bright and mild, and by ten o'clock the streets were full of people on foot, on horseback, and in wagons and carriages from the surrounding country going to the churches. Presbyterian and Methodist and Baptist and Episcopal, all large and handsome houses of worship, were thronged with people, and during the services a New England Sabbath stillness pervaded the place. All were filled and decorated with choice flowers. The platform of the Presbyterian church was bordered with several hundred fleurs-de-lis, while immense masses of calla lilies were banked around the organ rail, and the pulpit was wreathed with rose vines, bearing hundreds of choice and most fragrant flowers. This Sabbath was well kept at Pasadena, and all the churches were places of spiritual rest and joy.

## XIII

## THRIVING TOWNS

LOS ANGELES — A FLOURISHING CITY — HILLS AND HOMES — REDLANDS AND THE SMILEYS — THE BOY WHO WANTED TO BE A CIVIL ENGINEER

Los Angeles is the principal city in Southern California. It is a great business centre, and has been named as a possible capital of the state, if the seat of government should be removed from Sacramento. It has a population of sixty thousand, which is constantly increasing. It is substantially built upon a hilly region of country between the mountains and the sea, and about fifteen miles from each. Its broad and handsome streets are traversed by electric, and cable, and horse cars, the two former of which run over precipitous hills, and far out into beautiful suburbs. The private residences are prettily placed on handsome avenues shaded by palms and other trees, and usually have a well watered lawn about the house and rose-bushes and flowering plants around the piazzas. There is no ostentation or appearance of great wealth in the city, but many evidences of prosperity and comfort. The houses of well-to-do people of the middle class extend for miles from the centre of the town, all rendered easily accessible to stores and shops and churches and places of amusement by the swiftly running and well-appointed cars of the various street railways. Eleven steam railways centre at Los Angeles, of which two are competing trans-continental lines. A large ocean business is done through the ports of San Pedro, Santa Monica, and Redondo. The latter place is a great resort for recreation and sea-bathing, and possesses an excellent hotel. The merchants of Los Angeles do a large trade with the whole of Southern California, and the whole surrounding country produces in great abundance not only the vegetables and fruits needed by a large city, but enormous quantities of fruit, and much butter and cheese for export. The town has a river which is the source of much contention and even bloodshed. Like all California rivers, it has the very bad habit of breaking loose from its channel and flowing wild in the most unexpected directions. Many a house-lot and orchard have been swept away or covered thick with stones and gravel by this erratic stream. It now runs, for the most part, between banks of solid plank, but it resents such treatment, and has been known to get in behind the planking, and rip the whole barrier to pieces in a night. People who own property along the river, are at certain seasons in a strait betwixt their desire to irrigate and their fear of a flood; and quarrels about the use of the river, where it should go, and where it may not be permitted to run, are frequent.

In due time the whole matter of controlling these wild streams, husbanding the water for dry times,

ROSE COTTAGE, LOS ANGELES

and guarding against accident and ruin, will be reduced to a system in California. Something of this sort has been done at the new and beautiful settlement of Redlands in San Bernardino County, where the Smiley brothers have large holdings, handsome houses, and fruitful ranches. I made a pleasant excursion to the place, and was welcomed by Mr. Smiley with his usual courtesy.

The day was fine, with a cool air and a hot sun. One of my companions was a civil engineer who had lived many years in California, worked many of its mines and tramped over a large part of the state. He expatiated upon the beautiful regions yet undeveloped, and pointed out sections of country which would rival Redlands and Ontario if only capital was put into them. He knew of thousands of acres of woodland which would make the fortunes of purchasers, if they bought now, and built railways to bring the timber to a market. The conversation was interesting and very instructive when taken in connection with a subsequent interview with a small boy. This youth, about as big as a pepper-box, shared my seat for a while, and I asked him the usual question: "What are you going to be when you grow up?" He instantly replied, "Civil engineer." Doubting his knowledge, I said, "What does a civil engineer do?" As promptly as before, he answered, "He puts sticks into the ground for other folks, and says, 'Here's your land.'" That boy will get on in California. He has the correct idea of the "boom" which is the financial disease of our whole Western country. I subsequently learned that the boy's father was a painter, but he is far too clever for such a trade. He's going to be a civil engineer, and a future ruler in the Golden State.

There is still much land to be possessed in most of the towns of Southern California, though the towns are all laid out in lots, as if land were scarce. On some of the best streets in Pasadena the lots for sale were sixty feet wide by two hundred and twenty feet in depth. These were worth from five hundred to five thousand dollars and more, according to position. The prices were not materially different in other towns. Where the "boom" had struck and not expended itself, prices rose like the tide, only to recede in like manner; but the real-estate men claim that this tide rarely goes back to the point of beginning, and that there is a substantial gain in values after each time of excitement. Certainly this cannot be true of all the towns which have indulged in speculation, though it may be the case with those which are best situated and settled by solid people.

Redlands has been planted in a magnificent amphitheatre of mountains, far enough from the sea to escape the fogs of the coast, and upon hills which receive the reviving influences of the snow-clad ranges of mountains. The air is clear and pure and dry, the sun is hot but never dangerous, the water is clear as crystal, is stored in vast reservoirs in the mountains, and conducted by careful engineering to the town and through its orchards and gardens.

The Smiley place is called "Cañon Crest," from its position, which overlooks the gorge through which the Southern Pacific Railroad winds its way, and faces the gap in the mountains through which the Santa Fé Railroad enters into California.

The snow-clad range uplifts its huge mass of mountains in front of the rough hills which Mr. Smiley, at the cost of many thousands of dollars, has subdued and cultivated, and planted with fruit trees and shrubs and flowers. A beautiful valley lies below, through which the railway swings around in a loop, and in the far distance, on a clear day, the coast line and the shining waves of the great Pacific Ocean are visible at the horizon's limit. The snowy mountains, dark woods, and wild cañons contrast with cultivated slopes, beautiful meadows, and flower-gardens in a picture of natural loveliness, which is not rivalled even in this land of picturesque beauty. Mr. Smiley found this place — which once belonged to an old college friend of my own, for many years a missionary in California — in his journeys in behalf of the Indian tribes of our land. It is a fitting reward of his philanthropy, that he should own such a delightful winter ranch as one result of his labors. Our days in Pasadena and its neighborhood were filled with pleasures. But spring was advancing, and we were forced to leave one beautiful spot after another, not because their treasures were exhausted, but in deference to that foe to all idle travellers, *the plan of our journey*. Sometime I mean to travel without a plan.

## XIV

## SANTA BARBARA

BEAUTIFUL FOR SITUATION — AN EARTHQUAKE — THE TALE OF A PATRON SAINT — FIRST IMPRESSIONS — A PLACID TOWN — NATURAL BEAUTIES — A WINTER VIEW

SANTA BARBARA has been described as resting her head upon the Santa Ynez Mountains, and bathing her feet in the blue Pacific, and the description, though poetical, is accurate; for the town extends along a valley which lies directly between lofty mountains and a low line of hills, and reaches down to the sea. The main street of the town runs through this valley, from the beach to the foot-hills of the mountains.

The county, of the same name with the town, is a section embracing that part of the coast of California which runs east and west for about seventy miles, and is of a width of thirty-five miles from north to south. The exceptional climate of Santa Barbara is due to this curvature of the coast, to the parallel range of mountains which keep off the north winds, to a group of islands lying about twenty miles from shore, which shield it from ocean storms, and to warm currents of the Pacific. The southern part of the

SANTA BARBARA

county, forming the Santa Barbara valley, includes a number of smaller valleys or cañons, Carpinteria, Montecito, Goleta, and Ellwood, and contains somewhat more than one hundred thousand acres.

The ride from Los Angeles to Santa Barbara by rail is very beautiful. The latter part is along the ocean shore, and the views of the blue sea upon one side, and into green valleys decorated with masses of yellow and blue and pink flowers upon the other, were enchanting. One experience of the journey was novel and startling. The train, after passing through a long tunnel, was waiting the arrival of another train from Santa Barbara, and the passengers were lunching and walking around, when suddenly the cars rocked to and fro as if they were going at rapid speed on a curve, the chimney of the dining-room in the station at Saugus fell down, the glasses danced on the shelves and table, and everybody started with a nameless fear. Some thought an explosion had taken place, and others ascribed it to the wind, but residents of California recognized an undesirable acquaintance in the earthquake. Looking up towards the hills, little clouds of what seemed to be brown smoke were seen. In reality these were clouds of dust which rose from the crevices and fissures in the ground, caused by the seismic movement. The shocks were slight and lasted only a few seconds, but they were long enough to recall the Scripture: "He looketh on the earth and it trembleth; He toucheth the hills and they smoke."

There is a sketch of Santa Barbara, written from a strictly ecclesiastical point of view, by a Roman

Catholic priest, which gives with painstaking detail, a biography of Saint Barbara, from whom the town is named. She is said to have been a very beautiful daughter of a tyrannous Nicomedian, named Dioscorus, who was a satellite of the Roman Emperor Maximin. He hated and persecuted the Christians, and when his daughter, who had been taught by the famous Origen, implored him to have compassion on them, he discovered that she, too, had become a Christian. Full of fury, he threw her into prison. But, according to our author, Barbara "preferred a martyr's crown to a retraction of her vows and her religion." She was condemned to death, and while being tortured had a heavenly vision, and seemed to have passed away. But as she revived, her cruel father drew his sword and cut off her head, upon which lightning and thunder burst forth, destroying Dioscorus and the nefarious executioner. Father Gollell states that the head of Saint Barbara may be found preserved as a relic for veneration in the temple of All Saints in Rome, and that she is the patroness of artillery, "for if by flashes of flame and thunders the heavens defended her honor, with the booming and belching of cannon may they, too, repulse the attacks of unjust enemies." Thus far from the lives of the saints! The Spaniards evidently believed the tradition, and gave the saint's name to the lovely town, which has an ideal situation on the gentle slope between the stately mountains and the calm sea. The tops of these mountains in the winter sometimes have a crown of snow, in the spring the verdure is rich and velvety, and then a gray mantle covers the landscape.

Our first days in the place were disappointing. It was April, and we expected sunshine and warmth, but in their place we had fog and cold. After a few days of this sort the sun shone out, and thereafter mild airs and bright sunshine were the characteristics of the weather. Then we began to enter into the quiet beauty of the place, and to enjoy the serene influences which seemed to distil upon brain and nerves, from the deep blue sea with the dim outline of the distant islands, the restful strength of the verdure-clad mountains, and the fruitful hills and valleys near the town. Everything in Nature invited to repose and calm enjoyment. No noisy cars pervaded the streets; pavements, except one long stretch of smooth asphalt, are unknown; the daily train which came and went from the town, and the occasional arrival at the pier of a coast steamer, were the chief events. A wreck, twenty miles away, was the great excitement of our visit, and the rescued sailors, when they were brought to Santa Barbara, occupied the attention of the citizens for a week. The approaching floral festival gave pleasant occupation to residents and visitors, and simple enjoyments filled the passing days. We could have been content to live this calm, sweet life while months drifted placidly along, if there had been no calls from the outside world, and it was difficult not to envy the happy lot of some friends who had found here those earthly moorings which will not be slipped till they sail forth at the Master's bidding on that unknown sea which rolls round all the world.

We had been told that Santa Barbara would remind us of Nice, but the resemblance is slight. There is a curving shore, and a blue sea, and a mild climate, and the flowers and fruits which grow in such an atmosphere as both places possess. But there is none of the fashion and folly at the California resort which make Nice so attractive and exciting to those who love society and gayety. Santa Barbara is as simple in its life and manners as a New England village; there is no Monte Carlo near at hand to cast its baleful shadow over social life, and no foreign nobles to set an example of extravagance and dissipation to an indolent and yet restless community. There are none of the artificial improvements and expensive enjoyments which characterize the great resort of the Riviera to be found in this salubrious valley, where walks and drives and picnics are the healthful pleasures which occupy the time of residents and guests. The town has one long and wide street, which begins at the shore and ends in the midst of fields and gardens; and this is crossed at right angles by a number of other streets. These are shaded with rows of pepper and eucalyptus trees, and the houses stand in gardens and groves. The few stores, hotels, and churches are in the lower part of the place; and as the ground rises from the water, it is occupied with private dwellings, a few of which are built on separate hills, with some architectural elegance, and surrounded with choice gardens. Every garden has its wealth of shrubs and trees; roses and geraniums and heliotropes, which grow like moderate-sized trees, are formed into hedges, or trained as vines to cover the

CASTLE ROCK, SANTA BARBARA BAY

houses. Palms and camphor trees and shrubs, which in New York are nursed in green-houses, flourish on the lawns, and the greatest variety of fragrant flowers embower and beautify and perfume the place. These natural beauties are due, in large measure, to the evenness as well as to the mildness of the climate, and to the taste and cultivation of the inhabitants. The sun never smites the place with scorching heat; tornadoes and tempests, with desolating winds and lightning strokes, do not devastate the groves and gardens; even the rains, which come in torrents on some parts of the Pacific coast, fall more gently here, and winter is the loveliest part of the year, by the testimony of all who have lived in Santa Barbara from November to May. "This is the twelfth of January," writes a winter resident, "an average Santa Barbara day. Sitting in my room, with doors and windows open, I see ever blooming gardens in every direction, and hear the birds singing in the warm sunshine. Through my north window I see the foot-hills in their coat of verdure, while through my south window I see the grand old Pacific dotted with the Channel Islands, and the balmy sea-breeze brings with it the murmur of the waves as they break upon the hard sand of the broad beach a mile away. In the gardens in the immediate vicinity can be found lilies, heliotropes, fuchsias, carnations, and fifty other rare and beautiful flowers; three hundred different kinds of roses; almond trees with their snowy blossoms, and orange and lemon trees laden with their golden fruit. A stroll to the cañons would reveal myriads of delicately colored wild flowers, and the farmers could be seen turning the rich soil, making ready for planting."

This is a winter sketch of Santa Barbara, when the rains come sometimes for several days at a time, but generally in showers and at night, clearing off bright and warm during the day, so that in all the rainy season there are not more than ten or twelve rainy days. Then the hills are clothed with green, the landscape is aflame with the brilliant wild flowers, the birds sing their sweetest songs, and it is a delight to roam over grassy hills, explore wooded cañons, and sit and rest by the brook which flows from the mountain-side. Who would not rather spend winter in such a place than among the ice and snow of northern lands?

## XV

## ROMAN CATHOLIC MISSIONS

THE PADRES AND THEIR WORK — THE PRESIDIO AND THE CHURCH — HOW THE MISSIONS GREW — A SHORT, SAD HISTORY — THE LESSONS OF THE PAST

THE Spanish missions in California were organized from 1769, and were established chiefly in fruitful valleys along the coast from San Diego to Monterey. The fathers usually made their selections of sites in localities which had been previously chosen by the native Indians. They were led to do this by their appreciation of the knowledge which the natives had of the best parts of the country, and by their pious desire to be near to the settlements of those whom they desired to convert. Thus at San Diego, at San Juan Capistrano, at San Luis Rey, and San Gabriel, as well as at Santa Barbara, San Fernando, San Luis Obispo, San José, and Monterey, they built their massive adobe churches and monasteries, hung on wooden frameworks their sweet-toned Spanish bells, and began their work of tilling the soil and subjugating the Indians by their peaceful arts.

Most of the mission buildings in California were arranged in the form of a hollow square. The church building formed one side of the court or enclosure, and a long corridor supported by stone pillars and covered by a tiled roof, the other. The two remaining sides were made up of dormitories, storehouses, and workshops built against a high adobe wall. These buildings were a long time in construction, for there were few workers but unskilled Indians, who knew only how to build their own rude huts; and the wood used in construction had to be brought from the mountains miles away.

The chief feature of these buildings is their massive character, which shows that they were intended for places of defence, as well as for religious education. Most of these buildings are now in ruins, the open arches surround neglected court-yards overgrown with weeds and wild flowers, and some of the deserted rooms of the padres are used as stables for asses. The orchards and vineyards which the Catholic priests planted a hundred years ago are wild and unfruitful, and years of abandonment have destroyed these reminders of the early settlement of California, almost beyond restoration. To the artist who was our companion in travel, this outward ruin only made the missions more picturesque, and his paintings more valuable, and the younger members of the party found the moonlight more attractive in a dilapidated mission, than upon a hotel piazza. But it was sad to reflect upon such results from so much zeal and devotion. The padres are gone, and their work for the Indians of these regions seems like water spilled upon the ground; the missions are mostly falling to decay, and, with one or two exceptions, there is little promise that they will ever be revived or rebuilt.

BELFRY OF SAN GABRIEL MISSION

This conclusion is the sadder when we reflect that no arbitrary measures and no tyranny of conquest were employed to civilize and Christianize these people. The relation of the missionaries to the Indians was always paternal. They were, indeed, made to labor, and in time their position differed little from that of slaves, but they were willing slaves. They had cabins in villages near the missions, and were employed on large farms and vineyards and olive groves. Every morning they were gathered at sunrise in the church to hear mass, and then after breakfast they went forth to work. Following the Spanish habit, which is well adapted to the country, they rested three hours in the middle of the day, and then worked till an hour before sunset. Then the evening bell summoned the laborers to their supper and to another service. Thus the days passed in constant, but not exhausting, labor. The fathers taught them simple rules of faith and duty, exhorted them to industry and fidelity, and gave rewards to the best and most conscientious workers. The rule of the priests was beneficial so long as it lasted, but it left no permanent impress upon the people. A round of formal services, united with abundant exhortation, is not enough to lift a nation of heathen. The Indians knew that while the fathers were kind to them, it was that they might use them to enrich their order and enlarge their influence in the land. They gave them service for what they got, but few gave any love; and when the time of persecution came, they fell away from those who had proved themselves only selfish benefactors.

Carmel Mission at Monterey has been restored, and the Santa Barbara Mission has been repaired in recent years. The history of the latter is of interest, and it has been for a number of years a place of special attraction to the numerous strangers who spend their winters upon the California coast. Father Junipero Serra, whose name will always be held in sweet remembrance by the Catholics of California, chose Santa Barbara for a Presidio and Mission, and in April, 1782, he placed a cross there and blessed it. Four years later, in 1786, the foundation of a church was laid by his successor, which was not completed till 1794. The present structures were not all finished till 1820. The mission then stood in the midst of an Indian village; on one side was a large and well cultivated garden, and beyond a rich vineyard. Large and fertile farms, belonging to the Franciscans, stretched towards the sea and up the cañons into the mountains. From these mountains a stone aqueduct brought down the waters of a mountain stream, which was led through carved stone fountains in front of the church into a large and deep reservoir. There were bath-houses and gristmills and workshops supplied with water by the aqueducts, and storehouses for the many products of the orchards and fields. Statues of the saints and apostles ornamented the church, and numerous crosses were placed upon different parts of the building. Time has dealt ruthlessly with these decorations, and though the mission buildings are complete to-day, they are plain and unattractive. But the situation is unrivalled. From the piazza in front of the church, or, better still, from the belfry, a superb view of the mountains, the foot-hills, the lowlands, and the picturesque town, the beach, the blue channel of Santa Barbara, and the distant islands which form a kind of breakwater for the surges of the Pacific Ocean, can be seen to great advantage. Here, when the Angelus rings out for morning or evening prayer, a few priests dressed in coarse russet robes, with a cord around the waist, and sandalled feet, enter the church and go through a perfunctory routine of worship. At other times they milk their kine, and cultivate in a rude fashion the once beautiful garden, or they take male strangers through the building, and humbly accept the trifling fee which American charity bestows upon the successors of the rich and powerful order of Spanish priests who once ruled in luxury and pomp upon these shores.

The story of their downfall is a short one. In 1822 the Mexican government passed a law which set the Indians at liberty, and suspended the revenues of the priests. The act was repealed a year later, but the priests had taken the alarm, dismantled their churches, and fled. In 1833 the decree of secularization was passed. This converted the missions into secular curacies, leaving to the priests a house, and removing the fathers. Then the missions were handed over to commissioners, and the lands ordered to be colonized. In 1837 the usurping governor, Don Alvarado, plundered the missions, destroying some of them. A number of unsuccessful efforts were made to restore the clergy to their temporalities, and in 1842 the Pope made California a bishopric; while a year afterwards the governor of the state authorized the restoration of the missions. But most of the churches had been destroyed, many had been sold, the lands had passed into other hands, the day of the missions was over, and they are now only parish churches. The lesson is instructive. It is written all over the history of the Roman Catholic Church. It can be read in Rome itself, which within the memory of some of us was the intolerant, proud, and tyrannous capital of an ecclesiastical state. Wherever the Church turns from its legitimate work of preaching the Gospel and nurturing the flock of Christ, to aggrandize its ministers, to administer civil government, and to acquire political power, it parts company with its Great Founder, who said: "My kingdom is not of this world." Rome has never learned this text, and all her acquisitions, intrigues, and alliances, do but conduct her to an ultimate and disastrous downfall. In the days of her humble missionaries, she has often been an honored and useful instrument of divine Providence in leading people out of a gross darkness; but when in her pride and power she has sought to rule the nations, and make war in the name of Christ, ruin and desolation have come upon her.

Sitting on the low platform in front of the church, and gazing over the town to the sea, in the spring of the Columbian year, I have often thought how different would have been the history of our land, had the power of Spain or France fastened a Roman Catholic priesthood upon the territory of the United States; and have thanked God for the sturdy Protestantism which was permitted to found our institutions and secure our liberties. If we fully comprehended the blessing that we have received, and the dangers which we have escaped through such a providential guidance, we would be more vigilant and faithful!

## XVI

## FLOWER FESTIVAL AT SANTA BARBARA

MULTITUDES OF FLOWERS — TEN THOUSAND ROSES ON A CARRIAGE — A FLOWER DANCE — THE FLORAL PROCESSION — THE MAYOR'S PROCLAMATION

HORTICULTURE in the Santa Barbara valley is a profitable industry. Flowers grow here with a profusion and beauty in size and shape unknown elsewhere, flowering vines climb and cover trees fifty feet in height. Fuchsias have the proportions of trees, and beds of tulips and lilies and marigolds cover acres. The cultivated plants are manifold, and the wild flowers beyond enumeration. I have counted seventy different species collected in a morning walk, and the fields and mountain-sides are often purple with lupines, yellow with daisies, orange with the beautiful California poppies, deep blue with the wild onion blossom, or light blue with the lovely baby-blue-eyes. The common grass seems of a brighter shade of green, and the plumes of the feathery pampas nowhere wave with such grace and luxuriance.

It is not wonderful, then, that the residents of such a flower-garden should delight in floral displays, and that in the early spring, when Nature is most lavish of these favors, they should have a festival and dedi-

FLOWER FESTIVAL, SANTA BARBARA

cate some days to the floral deity. In 1893, the flower festival occupied four days, and every endeavor was made to make it more perfect and attractive than those which had preceded it. Exhibitions have been held for many years, but the first great festival was held when President Harrison visited the Pacific coast. This was so successful that it was determined to make it a yearly attraction at Santa Barbara. In 1892 the second festival brought a large concourse of visitors, and its success was complete. The profusion of flowers was overwhelming. Ten thousand fine roses were used in decorating a single vehicle. A long procession of carriages, hidden beneath masses of flowers, and filled with beautiful ladies in tasteful and appropriate costumes, made a charming scene. The festival was opened by a "dance of the flowers," in which twenty-eight young ladies, each personating a flower, entered in sets of four, and to soft music went through graceful movements. After their simple dance, they advanced to the platform, where were seated the invited guests, and laid at their feet garlands and wreaths.

In order to make the festival even more attractive the present year, the Flower Festival Association was organized. Its aim was not to make money, but to make the festival more beautiful, and all the receipts were used to make the floral display more complete; in short, to develop and foster a love for the beautiful. Prizes were offered for the most artistic decorations, and the most prominent people among the residents and visitors gave flowers and labor and enthusiasm, to produce a memorable festival. The shopkeepers entered into the plan with alacrity, and vied with each other in the decoration of their buildings and windows. One store was covered with calla lilies tastefully arranged in wire nets; another was hung with wreaths of oranges and lemons; others displayed columns of palm branches and arches of roses, exquisite arrangements of pampas plumes and fleurs de lis, and elaborate designs in all the colors of the floral treasury of the place. When the procession moved up State Street, it passed between rows of buildings adorned and decorated with flowers and fruits, an architectural vista such as was never seen in any town on earth before.

The procession had been preceded by a rose show and exhibition of flowers in the Pavilion, the chief assembly-room of the place. Besides the wonderful display of roses here, there were many beautiful and artistic combinations of plants and flowers which delighted the crowds of visitors for many hours. Another feature of the festival was a series of tournaments and games, and a flower festival ball, but the interest of the occasion centred upon the grand floral procession of decorated vehicles, and the battle of flowers, both of which took place upon the second day. The procession moved up State Street through the lines of decorated stores, to the upper end, where seats had been provided for about two thousand people. These were well occupied, and each party had brought huge baskets filled with small bouquets, with which to engage in battle.

First came the marshals on prancing steeds, whose saddles and bridles were covered thick with marigolds, or daisies, or purple Brodea, or roses, according to the owner's fancy. They were followed by a military band, which enlivened the occasion with frequent music. Next came a large float trimmed with roses and smilax, all of its sides being thus draped. On a bed of white flowers were four conch shells of pink roses, in which sat four little children representing the four seasons — Spring with a green dress and fruit blossoms; Summer in a pink dress, with roses to match; Autumn in a yellow dress, with fruit, red poppies, and grain; and Winter in a white dress, with swan's down and white pampas plumes. The next in order was an elegant float entirely formed of marguerites and cypress, and on this rested a boat completely covered with marguerites, as were also the oars and rudder, and the anchor and chain at the bow. Eight fine grays, with Russian collars of the same flowers, drew this device, which contained a charming family group.

A large Yosemite coach, drawn by six prancing black horses, was also decorated with these daisies, more than seventy-five thousand being used for the purpose. The harness and four outriders on gray horses were adorned in the same style. Following this was a farm wagon, whose sides were covered with the purple flowers of the wild onion. It looked like a mass of violets. Four snowy mules, trimmed with lilac and purple, drew this vehicle, which was filled with ladies and gentlemen dressed to represent Spanish peasants. Then came the *Monitor*, a boat made of calla lilies, its rail formed of wistaria, and a turret of Duchess roses. This turret revolved, and seven little lads in sailor costume kept up a constant fire of flowers, which was returned with interest by the spectators. A tropical scene represented the landing of Columbus. Palms and cacti and wild vines covered the island upon which Columbus was landing, and the whole effect was very realistic. There was a Washington coach of the olden time, with powdered dames and Continental soldiers inside, while the outside was hung with garlands of wistaria and Duchess roses, which blended with the tree moss that covered the coach panels. The wheels were solid with moss and great bunches of roses formed the hubs.

There was another coach trimmed with pampas plumes of white, and a calèche enveloped in similar plumes, dyed pink; a lovely phaeton covered with Beauty of Glazenwood roses, each wheel representing an immense rose; a surrey which was one solid mass of marigolds, drawn by two jet-black horses with marigold harnesses and reins; a carriage of calla lilies and green ferns; another covered with ivy and nasturtium vines interwoven; a wagonette entirely composed of white marguerites, in which rode a beautiful mother and three lovely children; a carriage of red geraniums, and another of red and white carnations. There were men and women on horses whose trappings were all made of wreaths and garlands, and men on bicycles covered with roses and daisies and marigolds. The decorations were in very great variety, and showed, in general, excellent taste.

For two hours, these gayly decorated equipages

moved up and down the promenade, and for most of this time the air was full of flying bouquets from spectators to exhibitors in a pleasant battle, till the roadway was as deeply covered with flowers as our Northern streets are with the driving snow in a winter's storm. At last the prizes were all assigned, the flower baskets were empty, and amidst cheers and congratulations, the beautiful procession broke up its line, and drove off to the various homes of the performers.

We have been in Nice at the annual battle of flowers, and also at Marseilles, and several times in Paris, but for profusion of flowers, variety and elaboration of design, and simple beauty, the Santa Barbara festival surpassed them all. It was a lovely sight, and as "a thing of beauty is a joy forever," it will always remain a pleasant memory among many others of this delightful town. Great crowds came to enjoy the festival from all parts of California, and many tourists arranged to be at Santa Barbara during this week. Every hotel was full to overflowing, and many private families had their houses full of guests. As there is still a rough element in California, the residuum of its population in the mining days, some apprehension is naturally felt in view of large and unusual gatherings. Such a feeling must have influenced the mayor to issue the following proclamation, which sounded strangely to our Eastern ears. Perhaps, however, the mayor knew better than we did what he was talking about: —

"NOTICE.

"MAYOR'S OFFICE,
"SANTA BARBARA, April 7, 1893.

" *W. W. Hopkins, Marshal of the city of Santa Barbara:*

"SIR: You will use every effort and means in your power and at your command, to keep out of Santa Barbara all confidence operators, thieves, thugs, house-breakers, sneaks, pickpockets, moll-buzzers, burglars, gopher-blowers, tramps, and their ilk.

"Should any of the above-enumerated characters get into the city, you will cause their immediate arrest, and hold until train time; then escort to the train with the admonition that, should they return, they will be given the butt end of the law. Should they return, arrest, and place against them a charge of vagrancy.

"In other words, if necessity demands, exceed your authority in giving protection to our people, and our officials and citizens will uphold you.

"You will use more than ordinary caution and diligence in having a general supervision over street fakirs.

"You will instruct your specials to give every protection, not only to citizens, but to guests and strangers within our city.

"You will instruct all specials to extend every courtesy to visitors; giving prompt aid when called upon, and immediate response to all information asked of them, keeping in mind that the very repu-

tation of our fair city is in your hands and in the hands of your officers.
"Respectfully,
"E. W. GATY, *Mayor.*"

I did not see a single "moll-buzzer," "gopher-blower," or "street fakir" in Santa Barbara during my whole sojourn there, and I attribute it to this proclamation, and wholesome fear of "the butt end of the law."

## XVII

## PLEASURE-DAYS AT SANTA BARBARA

THE MISSION CAÑON — A PICNIC AT ELLWOOD — MONTE CITO AND ITS GARDENS — THE HOT SPRINGS — THE OJAI VALLEY AND SAN MARCOS PASS

MANY delightful excursions can be made from Santa Barbara. Some of the pleasantest are those to the cañons, the heights of the Santa Ynez range, and the ranches whose hospitable proprietors make strangers and tourists welcome.

The nearest of these resorts is the Mission Cañon, which opens into the mountains just beyond the Mission. The road crosses the river, and then winds through liveoak and sycamore forests, over hills and ridges, following the course of that stream which was once used by the Franciscans for irrigation, and which now supplies Santa Barbara with water.

For the most part the valley is narrow and shut in, but sometimes there are outlooks when the foothills give way, and open the view over the fertile mesa or table-land and the beautiful blue sea. Now and then, level spaces and sheltered nooks, green with herbage or brilliant with flowers, are found along the road; in other places the hills rise precipitously among bare rocks, in whose crevices

OLIVE GROVE, COOPER'S RANCH

gnarled and twisted roots hold a few shrubs or tough cedars. As one climbs higher, the verdure gives place to bushes and brushwood, and higher still the mountains are bare and rocky. We were glad to have the cool shade of the oaks and sycamores to walk in, as we climbed up the cañon, delighting our eyes with the masses of purple lupines and delicate ferns and wild morning-glories which adorned the banks of the river; and were equally glad, when the walk was over, to sit in the sunshine and rest, breathing air laden with the perfume of the wild lilac and roses, and an infinite variety of plants and flowers. At the end of this cañon there is a picturesque waterfall, where the stream leaps seven times over ledges of rock from one pool to another, and pours down the smooth sides of the precipice in the midst of wild and rugged scenery.

One day, with a large and cheerful party of young and old, amateur photographers, water-color artists, botanists, and simple pleasure-seekers, we drove for a day's outing to Ellwood, known also as the Cooper ranch. This lies in a valley called "La Patera," which extends from Hope ranch to Gaviota Pass, and is bounded on the one side by the Santa Ynez Mountains, and on the other by the sea. The road lies along the hill-sides of Hope ranch, among which little Lake Fenton shines as a silver bowl. On either side of the road are neat houses, and yellow fields dotted with liveoak trees. The Hollister ranch occupies both sides of the road for several miles, and the house stands in a grove of fruit trees — oranges, lemons, almond, walnut, olive, peach, nectarine, and others. A large table-land is used for grazing, and the valleys which extend into the mountains are under careful cultivation. In the extensive gardens there is an avenue of palms, and a great variety of choice shrubs and plants. The "Glen Annie" palms are famous in the neighborhood, and the ranch is full of interest and instruction.

Ellwood, which joins the Hollister place, and which was our destination, comprises two thousand acres in fine condition. It lies along the road for a mile, but runs to the high foot-hills of the Santa Ynez, and down to the ocean beach. We drove through a long avenue of eucalyptus trees at the entrance, and then through winding roads bordered by orchards of various trees to the house and the gardens, which were filled with choice plants and innumerable roses and other flowers. The largest india-rubber tree that I have seen in California was growing here, and the Chinese gardeners were industriously watering and weeding the grounds. Then we passed into a grove of grand old oaks and wide-branching sycamores; near by were the mill where the olives are pressed and made into olive oil, the ovens for drying nuts, and the hives for honey; and not far off were the stables and packing-houses.

All this was upon the way to the entrance of the cañon, where, amid a grove of liveoaks, was our camping ground. The coaches were unloaded and the party dispersed, the artists to make sketches from points of vantage further up the cañon, the botanists to gather specimens for their herbariums, the youths and maidens to seek out shady and retired nooks, where they could repeat the sweet nothings which make young life so joyous, some to climb the hills and look upon the sea, and others to follow up the stream under the gray sycamore trees, till its course became too rough and steep for pleasure. In all such companies there is a home-staying and unselfish element, that spreads the festive tablecloth and arranges the welcome meal for the rest of the party. Such were some of us, and here in the grove beside a stream of fresh, cold water, with green foot-hills on one side, covered with waving fields of barley, and dark summits rising in another direction, and the winding avenues of blossoming trees just before us, the feast was prepared, decorated with manifold and choice bouquets, and made inviting to tired and hungry humanity by all those arts and devices which gentle ladies know. In pure air, mild but invigorating, blending the best elements of mountain and sea; with changing lights which made every hour a different scene, and delighted while it distracted the artist who tried to catch the atmosphere of the place; and with harmonious and intelligent company, we enjoyed the rest and refreshment and good cheer of one of Santa Barbara's choice places. For hours we rested here, and it was not until the westering sun and the cooler breeze told us that the day was waning that we sought our carriages and were whirled homeward by the fleet four-in-hands, whose equine thoughts centred chiefly about their commodious stables near the Arlington Hotel.

For a morning excursion, nothing is better than the drive to Montecito. From Santa Barbara, one may drive along the shore where the white surf line fringes the blue Pacific, and look far out on its swelling bosom beyond the dim forms of the rugged Channel Islands, till the haze conceals the immense solitary region beyond, or he may take the inland road to the little valley through vine-clad cottages and orchards. Along the slopes, where the bright green grass contrasts vividly with the dark foliage of the oaks, are many pretty cottages, and some pretentious villas, for the region is a favorite suburb of Santa Barbara, and is justly prized for its exceeding beauty. The southern part of the valley gently slopes to the sea, while on the north and west are the foot-hills, and above them the tall mountains wooded nearly to their tops. The valley is made up of many little vales, calm spots where one may woo seclusion and commune with Nature undisturbed. The largest ranch is at the entrance of the San Ysidro Cañon, and here there is an extensive orchard, and vineyards producing excellent grapes for wine. A boarding-house with half a dozen cottages has been established here, and in one of these we found Miss Susan Hale, of Boston, who claimed to be the discoverer of this lovely place. No one who can appreciate natural scenery and delicious climate would question her taste and judgment in such a choice, and, so far as I know, no one desires to contest her claim to the discovery. There are other spots not less beautiful, where all the resources of horticulture have been lavished to beautify the place. Here we saw many varieties of palms of great size and age; a sago palm from Ceylon; a silver tree, its leaves

OAK GROVE NEAR GAVIOTA

shining like burnished metal, from the Cape of Good Hope; a tea plant from China; india-rubber trees from South America; magnolia trees in bloom, and hedges of Chinese lemons along the garden walks. Beside these, there was an almost endless variety of choice trees and shrubs, and a huge grapevine near at hand large enough to shelter a goodly dinner-party.

Another day we climbed up the cañon to the hot springs. They consist of several hot sulphur and arsenic waters, about thirteen hundred feet above the sea, which have been known to the Indians for a long period, but were only brought to the notice of Californians in 1855. We bathed in the sulphurous waters and felt refreshed after a long scramble, and then rested and lunched on the little plateau by the hotel, where we overlooked lovely Montecito, and watched with interest the San Francisco steamer as she came down the coast and made fast to the Santa Barbara pier. The hills among which we strolled were full of holes, from which, our guide said, rattlesnakes might be expected when the weather grew warmer, so that this Eden has a real snake. A young entomologist also showed me some very large tarantulas impaled upon a long needle, and one or two of the curious mud boxes with a trap-door at the top, in which these venomous and disagreeable spiders live. After such views of insect life, we were careful about sitting on banks, even if wild thyme did grow there, and preferred a hard chair to a lounge upon a flowery mead.

Time and space would fail to enumerate the charming places which court the attention of the tourist. Some of our associates went through the Ojai valley, and were extravagant in their praises of the wonderful beauties of "Oak Glen," where the boughs of the trees form gothic arches; and others went to Santa Clara, the home of "Ramona;" and others of a more practical turn investigated the oil wells in Wheeler's Cañon, near Ventura. We were content with nearer excursions, and with one long and delightful day on the San Marcos Pass, over which the road runs to San Luis Obispo and Monterey. This was indeed a day of rare enjoyment in pleasant company, far up on the mountains, in the pure, dry air and sparkling sunshine, with a dozen wild cañons beneath and around us, lower down the cultivated foothills and the ranches of which I have written, then the mesa or sloping table-land, the villages and the azure ocean in the distance. I have seen nearly all the winter resorts of California, and though I have heard of fogs, and have felt chilly winds and variable weather at most of them, Santa Barbara and its surroundings do most commend themselves to me. When winter winds again begin to blow, I shall draw the curtains, and put another log upon my costly wood fire, and shutting my eyes, shall dream of the peaceful and sunny slopes of the Santa Ynez, and the happy and well-kept town which lies at its base. Perhaps the dream may prove a reality after all.

# XVIII

## ANCIENT SPANISH HOUSES

CARRILLO ARGUELLO AND DE LA GUERRA — OLD DAYS IN SANTA BARBARA — FEASTS AND WEDDINGS — THE CHINESE COLONY — FRIENDS AND THEIR WORK

THERE is one part of Santa Barbara which seems out of harmony with its present life. It leads one back into the old Spanish times, when the red-tiled adobe houses were built, and the Castilians dwelt in dignity and power on the California coast. This place is but a stone's throw from the main street of Santa Barbara, and Governor Carrillo's house may still be seen on State Street. It is a long, low structure with a broad foundation of solid stone, and a broad and cool veranda, where one might swing at ease in a comfortable hammock. The outside walls of the house are three feet thick, and the inner divisions are at least two feet through; the window-seats are as wide as the thickness of the walls, and the low-studded doors have broad and ample thresholds.

All the rooms in this house are large, being wide and long, although the ceilings are low. The doors and windows are small, and the latter have heavy wooden shutters. The floor was formerly of earth, but use had made it as hard and smooth as stone.

The walls were trowelled even, and red cedar window frames carefully set in them. The lower rooms only are used, and the upper story exhibits the huge adobe bricks and immense wooden tree trunks in their natural state used for beams. These were laid across from wall to wall to form the roof, and bound together with rawhide thongs which show no signs of decay after ninety years. Over the beams is a layer of brush, and over that the tiles, which were made and burned close at hand. After all these years, this primitive building stands tight and strong.

A part of the Carrillo House is used for a dwelling, and the rest is occupied by the National History Society. Here Spanish and Indian relics are preserved, but, after all, the house itself is the main feature of attraction. Some of its windows are glazed, while others have only rows of iron bars, like the lower stories of the houses in Spain. The walls of one room were covered with frescoes on a ground of white plaster, a Moorish design. General Frémont arrived in Santa Barbara in December, 1846, and made this house and the adjoining one his headquarters, because it was the largest, and in better condition than any other.

The other house which General Frémont used was built by Captain Arguello, who succeeded Carrillo. He was made governor-general of California in 1815, having been for many years commandant of the Presidio. His house was one of the finest in old Santa Barbara, containing thirty rooms, and was the only residence which completely enclosed a large

OLD ADOBE, SANTA BARBARA

square in the style of the Spanish patio. The woodwork was of Spanish cedar, and one of the door frames, which is used in a shed near by, is richly carved in a design of fluted columns.

The court-yard tempted Frémont to use it as an enclosure for his animals. They had no regard for the former owners or their traditions, and soon reduced the building to ruin, and now only a heap of dilapidated adobe and some few carved beams remain.

After Captain Arguello, came Captain José de la Guerra, who held office for many years, during which time Mexico became independent of Spain. He was of a good Castilian family, and built the house where the de la Guerra family still live, while he was the commander of the Presidio. .The house was outside of the grounds, and had a chapel, whose statues and paintings are still preserved in the parish church. The bell tower has fallen down, but the bells were rehung upon frames, and still call the worshippers to matins and vespers.

Captain de la Guerra built this house in 1823. It extends for one hundred feet on three sides of a square, with a broad piazza and three wide flights of steps. The roof is supported by slender adobe pillars, the whole house being made of the same sundried bricks plastered on the outside. The ends of the house have broken somewhat, and are covered with wood for protection, but the rest of the building is in excellent condition.

In the old days, these court-yards and verandas and rooms were the scene of lavish hospitality. The guests assembled and danced on the piazzas and in the court-yard on every day for a whole week. Everybody was asked, and all were made welcome to the feast which was spread for all under the shade of the portico, or of the trees and vines. The relatives were entertained in the salon, and the week of gayety was long remembered. It is of this family that Richard H. Dana speaks, in his "Two Years before the Mast," when the mansion was not large enough to hold the guests bidden to the wedding of Doña Anneta de la Guerra, the youngest daughter of the grandee of the place, who married the agent of the owners of the *Pilgrim*. The steward was ashore three days making pastry, guns pealed out salutes, and flags were run up, and the vessel was dressed in colors, and a boat's crew rowed the officers ashore. A few words from his journal will be of interest: "At ten o'clock the bride went up with her sister to the confessional, dressed in deep black. Nearly an hour intervened, when the great doors of the mission church opened, the bells rang out a long discordant peal, the private signal for us was run up by the captain ashore, the bride, dressed in complete white, came out of the church with the bridegroom, followed by a long procession. Just as she stepped from the church door, a small white cloud issued from the bows of our ship, which was full in sight, the loud report echoed among the surrounding hills and over the bay, and instantly the ship was dressed in flags and pennants from stem to stern. Twenty-three guns followed in regular succession, with an interval of fifteen seconds between each, when the cloud cleared away, and the ship lay dressed in her colors all day. At sundown, another salute of the same number of guns was fired, and all the flags run down. This we thought was pretty well — a gun every fifteen seconds — for a merchantman with only four guns and a dozen or twenty men.

"After supper the gig's crew were called, and we rowed ashore, dressed in our uniform, beached the boat and went up to the fandango. The bride's father's house was the principal one in the place, with a large court in front, upon which a tent was built, capable of containing several hundred people. As we drew near, we heard the accustomed sound of violins and guitars, and saw a great motion of the people within. Going in, we found nearly all the people of the town — men, women, and children — collected and crowded together, leaving barely room for the dancers; for on these occasions no invitations are given, but every one is expected to come, though there is always a private entertainment within the house for particular friends. The old women sat down in rows, clapping their hands to the music, and applauding the young ones. The music was lively, and among the tunes we recognized several of our popular airs."

These scenes have passed away, never to return; the house still stands, and the family still lives there. Around the house, and for a long distance towards Montecito, were the gardens of the estate. This was one of the most fertile parts of the whole valley, well watered and productive. The gardens were for pleasure as well as profit, with all sorts of fruit trees and many flowering plants along the winding paths. Little now remains of these gardens of delight except the palms and cacti, and an occasional orange tree. The family are proud of their lineage, and have occupied many important offices and trusts. The builder and his son are buried here, and the third generation dwell in Santa Barbara.

This grand old house is surrounded with small and mean dwellings. These were built for soldiers and Indians, and are now occupied by the Chinese, who have invaded Spanishtown, erected their Joss in one of the adobe mansions, and have occupied others as shops. Their red posters flame in the windows, and the sickening odor of their opium pipes pervades the little rooms where they congregate. They are not all heathen, for we attended the anniversary of the Presbyterian Chinese Mission School on an April Sabbath evening, and listened to a most interesting programme of recitations, songs, and original addresses by Louis Fon, Tang Ting, Lee Ling, Gen Yan, Quon Woon, Pon Sam, and other members of the school under charge of Mrs. Bell. Rev. Dr. Carrier conducted the exercises, and Mrs. Cheung Wong played the organ and led the music. Some of the speeches showed marked ability, and the school is a successful one. It is a good work, and will help to counteract the heathenism of the rest of the Chinese population.

## XIX

## HOW WE WENT TO YOSEMITE

THE CROWN OF CALIFORNIA SCENERY — A WILY AGENT — RUTS AND BOGS — FINE AIR AND HARD FARE — AN AMERICAN JOLTING CAR — MULES AND THEIR DRIVERS — THE PUBLIC AND ITS SERVANTS

THE most exhausting, expensive, and impressive excursion which the tourist in California can make is doubtless that to the Yosemite Valley. When made in the early spring, it is said to be a rougher but more remunerative trip than later on. In the old days of staging and horseback riding, this journey would have been only an incident in the usual course of pounding, jolting, and stowing which our fathers went through when they travelled by public conveyance, and which some of us can remember as items in our childhood. But such an excursion in these days of Pullman cars and palace hotels is, to say the least, a novelty. Until within a few years, the Yosemite Valley had the monopoly of the sightseers in the far West. One who crossed the Rockies, and did not climb down into the rock-ribbed valley through which the river Merced runs, made a most important omission, for painters and quill-drivers had so advertised the wonders and beauties of Yosemite, that it was believed to be one of the greatest sights in the world. Since the discovery of other cañons in Colorado and Arizona, and the opening of the Yellowstone Park, the pilgrimage to Yosemite has somewhat declined, though it is still a famous resort, especially for Englishmen and for American excursionists.

Under ordinary circumstances, its grandeur and beauty ought to repay the strong and enthusiastic traveller for the rough riding and tough fare which are the conditions of his visit.

We were in San Francisco about the first of May, and were politely informed by the childlike and bland agents of the only route by which the valley is accessible at such a date, that the roads were in fine condition, the snow all cleared away, the hotels ready for business, and that we would be more troubled with sun and dust than with snow and mud upon our journey. The five feet of snow which we afterwards passed through upon our road, the deep ruts and quagmires in which the coaches and horses plunged and wallowed, and the one cow in the valley, which must have been fed chiefly upon ice-water, somewhat shook our confidence in the agent's veracity, and added to the surprises of the excursion. But the superb air from the pine forests on the mountains, the enchanting scenery of the valley, and the company of ladies and gentlemen, who for the most part made light of their miseries and privations, went far to reconcile us to the deceptive conditions under which we made our entrance. With some seasoned travellers, and a merry party of young people, we

YOSEMITE VALLEY FROM UNION POINT

made our journey. It was long, rough, cold, and hard, but it will always be a memorable portion of our California pilgrimage, and grow more delightful as distance lends enchantment to the view, and as the infelicities and trials of the way fade out of sight, and leave only the grand features and pleasant incidents of the visit.

On a fine afternoon we rode from San Francisco to Berenda, a station on the Southern Pacific Road, where we anchored for the night. During the night, the train of a New York millionaire and another private car pulled up alongside, and in the morning, bright and early, the trains started off for Raymond, the last point of the railroad ride, and where coaches are to be taken for the journey to the valley.

The conditions which make it easy to whirl a train of parlor cars along the New York Central, do not exist upon the railroad line between Berenda and Raymond. This road winds, and climbs, and dodges around and about, over and among hills and valleys, the grades being steep and the curves sharp. It was not wonderful, therefore, that the aristocratic coaches with their large-wheeled engines soon got stalled upon the heavy up-grades, and were compelled to call upon the more practical freight engine to help them over the road. At last, however, we were all at Raymond, breakfasted, and were distributed in coaches. Eleven persons and a driver are a load for each coach, and four horses or mules are allotted to draw each company. The coaches are single-deck vehicles of the old Concord thoroughbrace and axle pattern, some of them open, and others supplied with a canopy. They are very stout and heavy, and probably are among the hardest riding vehicles ever invented by man. Every stone which the wheels run over leaves its impress upon the passenger, the ruts of the road sway the weighty carriage like a ship in a heavy sea, the waterbars along the course throw the rider from his seat as surely as a bronco does, and the high wheels scatter dust and mud upon the inmates of the coach without distinction of position, age, or sex. The box seat beside the driver is the most desirable place, but when three occupy it, the iron rail does more than protect the outside passenger, while the middle one becomes intimately acquainted with the elbows of the driver and the butt end of his whip-handle.

If the Jehu is an old-stager, his stock of information, stories, and jests makes up for many side thrusts and squeezes, and helps to pass the hours when the lumbering vehicle creeps up hills, or rattles and jumps down the steep inclines, often frightfully near the edge of a precipice.

The "swells" managed to get most of the good horses, so quiet people were provided with mules, and my respect for these animals increased during this trip. They can take more beating with less result than any other beasts. Indeed, it became a question, now and then, which of the two worked the harder, the driver or the mules.

The sky was clear, the air chill, the waysides literally carpeted with yellow and blue and purple flowers; wild white lilacs, and the lovely manzanitas sending out a rich fragrance, and the bay bushes adding their refreshing perfume. The prospect of hill and vale widened every hour, as we rose higher and higher, and the barometer began to mark the thousands of feet which we had climbed above the level of the sea. All day the teams toiled along, each one doing its duty under lash and voice for eight or ten miles, and then giving place to another. Late in the evening we arrived at Wawona, where a large house, well situated, offers accommodations to guests. It was overcrowded, and late comers took what they could get, but all were hungry enough to eat the abundant supper which was provided, and after roasting themselves before a huge log fire, were ready to lie down in the cold beds, and sleep as only the weary can. At break of day the travellers were again summoned, not because they were in a hurry to get on, but because the coaches were to make one trip into the valley, and another out of the valley within the twelve hours. There is altogether too much of this style of business in this country. Trains and boats and coaches are run, not for the comfort and convenience of passengers, but to suit the fancies of superintendents, or the economies of the company. The American public is the most long-suffering in the world, and pays large prices to be dictated to and overrun by those who ought to be its servants. From the railway porter, who treats the ordinary traveller with contempt, up to the president of the company, who takes the right of way on a road of which he is only the head servant, and through every branch of public service, the people are treated as inferiors, and as possessing few rights which officials or corporations are bound to respect. My regard for some of the institutions and customs of what we sometimes call "effete civilizations" is increased every time I travel in my own country. The nobility of respectful, efficient, and intelligent service impresses itself upon one who marks its woful lack in this free and mighty independent land, for it is far more honorable to do a humble duty well than to swagger in a station whose duties are regarded as servile simply because they demand quietness, courtesy, and obedience. These ideas are not much in harmony with the spirit of the age, which is pushing, boisterous, intolerant of criticism, and reckons it important to protest against service as derogatory to manhood.

Arising, a long time before the sun, we hurried through breakfast to accommodate the driver who wanted to "make time," and were off. Through mud and snow, over rough and bad roads, we were jerked and jolted for five weary hours, and then, through the white veil of a feathery snow-storm we caught our first view of Yosemite, with its crags and battlements, its rushing river, and its resounding and beautiful waterfalls. When the flurry of snow ceased, and the sun shone out, the mingled grandeur and beauty of the scene drew exclamations of delight and enthusiasm from every lip; the weariness of the way was almost forgotten, as the horses whirled the coaches around the sharp curves, and then five miles over the level floor of the valley, amid ever increasing wonders, to the hotel at the upper end. Here we were to rest for some days among the sublime and glorious works of the great Creator.

## XX

## THE YOSEMITE VALLEY

OUR ENTRANCE — WONDERFUL VIEWS — MANIFOLD AND BEAUTIFUL WATERFALLS — PRECIPICES THOUSANDS OF FEET HIGH — MIRROR LAKE AND MERCED RIVER — DID THE 'BOTTOM DROP OUT — GRANDEUR AND TRIVIALITY

IT was afternoon of the second day of stage-riding, and the third day from San Francisco, before we reached the Yosemite Valley. Though the route was full of varied interest, there was an amount of physical pain and privation, of cold and hunger, connected with the transportation, that made us rejoice that the end of our pilgrimage was near. On we drove through the forests of mighty trees. The air was full of fleecy and feathery snow, which contrasted with the dark foliage of the evergreens. A sudden turn in the road brought us to the steep side of the great Yosemite Valley. Gusts of wind drifted the snow-clouds back and forth, now revealing and anon concealing the opposite side. For a few moments the snow ceased, the sun shone out, and we caught our first view from Inspiration Point of the falling waters, and towering rocks, and deep ravines, and tree-covered heights, which mingle here in a wonderful and beautiful picture. Then the snowy veil was dropped again, and as we jumped and jolted down the mountain-side, this veil swung back now and then, giving glimpses of grandeur and beauty all along the route. Soon we were below the snow-clouds, and drove among green trees and grassy meadows, and beside the pure waters of the Merced as it hurried down the cañon.

The Yosemite lies in the heart of the Sierra Nevada Mountains about one hundred and fifty miles due east from San Francisco. Its Indian name means, "full-grown grizzly bear," and has no special application to the valley. The valley is distinguished from all other valleys by its enormous depth, the perpendicular walls which enclose it, and by the small amount of débris at the base of these walls. It seems as though it must have sunk down suddenly from the midst of the table-lands which surround it. But conjectures are vain. Whether it was washed out by the streams, or ground out by the ice mills of the glacial period, or whether the bottom fell out, and where it fell to, and what made the hole that the bottom fell into, are all points that have been carefully discussed, but never settled. But the fact remains that here is a valley, wonderful not only in depths and heights, but in its carved, water-quarried recesses and mountain walls, that exhibit new beauties in every receding angle and cloud-supporting buttress.

During the spring and early summer, when the yet deep snows of the high Sierra are melting rapidly, there are many waterfalls pouring down the precipitous sides of the valley. As the season advances, several of these cataracts dwindle away until they become almost imperceptible trickles of water. One who has only seen these torrents in their full and majestic flow can with difficulty comprehend their almost total disappearance. And one who looks on their shrunken proportions in the late autumn has even more difficulty in picturing to himself the captivating spectacle presented by the falls in their season of power and splendor.

Our first object of interest, when we reached the valley floor, was the Bridal Veil Fall. The road comes close beside it. A stream of water flowing through meadows and forests from a lake thirty miles away, comes to the precipice with a width of forty feet, and a depth that varies with the season of the year. It leaps over the precipice and falls in filmy folds down, down, nine hundred feet, upon rocks and foaming waters. The wind floats out the wreaths of spray, and in the afternoon rainbow circles form in the hanging clouds of vapor, and the whole place sparkles and gleams in the sunlight. Just opposite the Bridal Veil Fall is a narrow band of water falling down the rocky wall of the valley which is called sometimes The Ribbon, at other times Widow's Tears, because it quickly dries up after the snows have melted and Fall Creek, a tributary of the Merced River, runs low. As we looked at the stream pouring over the face of the rock, it could be compared to nothing better than delicate lacework, though the glass showed that there was a great amount of water falling.

Alongside the road, just beyond, are the Cathedral rocks, which bear a striking resemblance to the Gothic piles of England. Portions of these massive towers, which rise twenty-seven hundred feet from the valley, have fallen, and lie scattered in massive fragments at the base, and huge fissures in the rocky pinnacles give evil omen of similar disasters. As we look across the green and swiftly flowing Merced, above the Widow's Tears, the immense mass of El Capitan rises, forming the North wall. It is by far the most imposing feature of the valley, four thousand feet high, of a cream-colored stone, a sheer and incurving precipice from base to top. The plants and herbage which find a place everywhere in the valley are so small upon El Capitan that the impression is produced of a simple stone structure, vaster than the sphinx or the pyramids. It is the giant of the place, a grand and glorious mountain of solid stone. On the same side are three lofty and immense pillars of granite, the highest of which equals El Capitan in altitude. They are appropriately named, Three Brothers, for the sons of the oldest of the Yosemite chiefs, Tenaya. They keep watch with El Capitan upon the north, while opposite, the Sentinel stands three thousand feet high, forming one of the finest features of the whole region. By a curve in the valley, the Sentinel is brought into its centre, and from either part he stands majestic, lofty, and grandly formed, the guardian of this wonderful treasure-house of Nature. From the base of the Sentinel, the finest waterfall, which gives name to the valley, is seen to great advantage. The

BRIDAL VEIL FALL, YOSEMITE

Yosemite River flows through granite walls, from the lofty heights where snow lies more than half the year, till it comes to the precipice far above the forest line, where it pours over a deep and powerful stream, which falls into a broad basin, boils for a moment, and then plunges down, to repeat its action once more before it reaches the valley. The first fall is a sheer descent of one thousand five hundred feet, but the whole height from summit to base is two thousand six hundred feet. From some points in the valley the three leaps seem merged in one vast mass of milk-white foaming water, and seen in the moonlight the effect is beautiful beyond description. It is a favorite excursion, to climb by circuitous and zigzag paths to the top of the precipice, and if the wind be from the right quarter, so that one is not drenched with spray, the views into the recesses of the cataract are exciting and wonderful. One of the numerous writers upon the place, after saying that "Yosemite Falls by moonlight is a scene no artist dare attempt to paint, no pen to describe," proceeds to quote as follows: "As the night queen rides out and a faint bar of light spans the chasm of the domes upheld by shadows almost a mile high, she touches gently the great falls of the Upper Yosemite, transforming the falling crystals into meteors of burnished silver, which the night wind whirls in wild, fantastic wreaths against the frowning cliffs." That is just about as we saw it by the light of a full moon.

The view from the Sentinel point, up and down the valley, is magnificent. The northern view is closed by Cloud's Rest, a lofty pile of granite which rises six thousand feet into the sky, and upon its awful summit there is often a fleecy cloud, which gives name to the mountain; nearer at hand are the North Dome, Royal Arches, and Washington Column, on the left, and Glacier Point, with its dizzy promontory, on the right; while between the two the graceful Half Dome rises nearly five thousand feet into the heavens.

At the other end of the valley there are beautiful cascades, and the drive from Mirror Lake, where the huge mountains are pictured in all their grandeur on a calm day, down one side of the valley to the cascades, and up on the other to the Stoneman House, is never to be forgotten. Though Yosemite is chiefly famous for the number and beauty of its waterfalls, yet the walls which shut it in are so stupendous in height and grandeur, and so varied and wonderful in their outlines, and so harmonious in their relations to each other that no one can look long upon them without feeling their awful power. Reverence for that which is so high and grand insensibly grows upon the men whose soul is open to impressions, and as excursions are made to Union and Glacier points, to the Nevada and Vernal falls, and into the recesses of the mountains, the sense of the sublimity and glory of these works of God is deepened and strengthened.

It is pitiful, in the midst of such sublime scenes, to descend to the trivialities of ordinary experience, and think so much of what kind of an ass one can get to ride on to the Vernal and Nevada falls, whether there will be enough milk to go around at table, and how many trout will be served at supper; but all travellers know that, even in the presence of the grandest and most glorious works of God, the mind of the average man does not commune with its Maker unless these sordid questions are settled. Our case was no exception to the rule. The hotel was very crowded, there was only one private room with a fireplace, a solitary cow gave all the milk, and the trout had no appreciation of how much they were wanted. Yankee smartness and New York extravagance vied with Chicago bluster in the effort to come out ahead in the various problems of food, accommodation, and transportation, and the modest men and women, who only wanted their fair share of comforts and blessings, were often poorly served, or not served at all. The rule, "every one for himself," has its best illustration in such travels, and yet I have known people who were very happy because they had been able to prefer the comfort and convenience of others to their own, and such were some of those who went to the Yosemite and spent the week with us there.

## XXI

## CALIFORNIA BIG TREES

MARIPOSA AND SANTA CRUZ GROVES — COMPARISONS AND MEASUREMENTS

WE were sorry to leave the Yosemite Valley for two reasons. One was because it was unlikely that we should ever look again upon those grand walls of rock, those beautiful waterfalls, the lakes that mirror the mountains, and the dark, green river of pure water that flows through the verdant floor of the valley. These things will be for memory to rest upon and rejoice in through coming years, but they will not be like the oft-repeated views of Niagara and the White Mountains, nor even familiar friends as Mount Blanc and many scenes of the Swiss Alps.

The other sorrow at leaving the valley was prospective. A vision of future misery was before us. There stood the red instrument of torture at the door, with its huge wheels, and awful thorough-braces, well named "rack," and falsely named cushions, as hard as excelsior and leather could make them. And there, too, sat the hardened sinner who was to propel this barbarous construction over rock and rut, and log and stone, through bog and snow and flooding rivers, for the next two days. He sat firmly, as if made of cast-iron, with his sceptre, a long-lashed whip, in his hand, ready to beat recalcitrant or despairing beasts into a sense of their duty or a comprehension of their misery. We said farewell to friends, entered the chariot, and climbed the rugged mountain, lingering a moment at Inspiration Point, and then braced ourselves for the unmitigated punishment of the next two days. There was to be one interval of pleasure, in a new sight, and to that we hopefully looked forward. The warm weather and a gang of shovellers had opened the road to the Mariposa "Big Trees," and we knew that they were well worth seeing. We slept at Wawona, sad and sore after our rough ride, but responded to the thundering process by which we were awaked in the morning. It reminded me of the answer which the stout, black stewardess of a Fall River boat once made to my innocent inquiry, whether passengers were waked to take the railroad train? With much feeling she replied: "We calls the parties, and pounds on the doors, and rings a gong, and them that sleeps after that is fortinit."

In the gray morning we wound up the steep road for several hours, until we came to the turning which led to the Big Trees. It is a ride of two hours up to the grove, and the snow was from three to five feet deep the last part of the way. My readers will remember that this excursion was made early in the month of May. By the middle of June it would be difficult to find a snow-bank in the most sequestered part of the grove.

"How shall we know when we come to the Big

Trees?" asked the eager aspirant for knowledge who accompanies every party. "You'll know 'em when you see 'em," was the laconic reply of the mule driver; and so we did; the great red and black monsters needed no introduction. There they stood, these giants of the forest, as they have stood for thousands of years. Fires have roared and blazed about them and burned their trunks and branches, and literally disembowelled some of them so that you can look up through them as through a tall chimney, but their upper branches are full of life, and green tufts of leaves crown their tops. The ice and snow of a thousand winters have wrapped them around in chilly embrace, and furious tempests have torn off immense limbs, but neither fire, nor frost, nor winter's furious storms, nor summer's glowing heat, have done aught but reveal their sturdy strength, their majestic and awe-inspiring character. They have been named for states which are infants in age compared with them, and for great generals whose names will be forgotten long before these massive trunks decay and their towering pinnacles are levelled in the dust. They are the creations of One who is without beginning of days or end of life; and more than any living and growing thing that I have seen upon the face of the earth, they seem to partake of the divine element of unchanging and continuous existence. It is solemnizing to stand in the presence of living creatures which have existed ever since Moses climbed into Sinai and communed with the invisible God; to see a growing crown of vigorous leaves and branches on the head of a giant who was

BIG TREES, SANTA CRUZ

a forest king when David reigned in Zion; to wind a cord around a tree until it measures ninety-four feet, and then to look up along the body of this Grizzly Giant, beside whom Goliath would be an insect, and see his red right arm branch out six feet in diameter, eighteen feet around, at the height of nearly two hundred feet.

Figures give little idea of the size, and pictures only an imperfect impression of the shape and coloring and grandeur of these trees. When I say that, the snow being cleared away, a four-horse coach could be driven through the living body of the tree called Wawona, and that many of the trees are larger at the base, and a hundred feet higher than the Bunker Hill Monument, some comparisons may be made. There are higher trees than these in Australia, but none that combine girth and height like the Sequoia Gigantea, of the Mariposa and Calaveras groves.

Mr. John Muir, who knows as much as any one of the Big Trees, says of them: "There is something wonderfully telling and impressive about Sequoia, even when beheld at a distance of several miles. Its dense foliage and smoothly rounded outlines enable us to recognize it in any company, and when one of the oldest patriarchs attains full stature on some commanding ridge, it seems the very god of the woods. Full-grown specimens are about fifteen or twenty feet in diameter, measured about the swelling base, and about two hundred and fifty feet high. Trees twenty-five feet in diameter are not rare, and one is now and then found thirty feet in diameter, but very rarely any larger. The grandest specimen that I have measured is a stump about ninety feet high, which is thirty-five feet eight inches in diameter, measured inside the bark, above the bulging base. The wood is dull purplish red in color, easily worked, and very enduring, lasting, even when exposed to the weather, for hundreds of years. Fortunate old trees, that have passed their three thousandth birthday, without injury from lightning, present a mount-like summit of warm yellow-green foliage, and their colossal shafts are of a beautiful brown color, exquisitely tapered, and branchless to a height of a hundred and fifty feet. Younger trees have darker, bluish foliage, and shoot up with tops comparatively sharp."

In the lower grove, which we first entered, there are about one hundred fine trees, and here stands the "Grizzly Giant." The upper grove contains three hundred and sixty-five big trees, and in that grove stands the "Chimney," burned through from base to point, and yet living and branching; and the tunnelled tree, through whose heart, as I have said, the stage road has been cut. This tree is twenty-seven feet in diameter, and the road which passes through it is ten feet wide.

The bark of the Sequoia, which is sometimes two feet thick, is of a dark, rich cinnamon tint, and is channelled toward the base with vertical furrows. The cones, which mature in about five years, are about the size and shape of a turkey's egg.

Sequoia Sempervirens, or the redwood of the Coast Range, is a near relative of the Gigantea, but they are never found together; the latter is found in the region of the Sierra Nevada only, and the former on the Coast Range. The redwood is one of the handsomest forest trees of California, and the Big Tree Grove, near Santa Cruz, is the finest single group of trees in California.

We had visited these before we went to the Yosemite, and were, therefore, in a measure prepared for the sight of the Mariposa giants, but the largest of the Santa Cruz trees is but seventy feet in circumference. In one of these, a tree called the "Giant," three hundred feet high and twenty-one feet across, General Frémont camped for several days, in 1847, and there is an interesting photograph of the general and a family party, hand in hand, as they formed a circle around this tree many years after. It took thirteen full-grown people, with outstretched hands, to encircle the tree, and the number does not seem to have been unlucky to the tree or the measurers.

A fine specimen of a trunk made of genuine bark was on exhibition at the Chicago Fair, and also a pavilion made of the wood from San Mateo County. The wood is plentiful in smaller growth, is easily worked, finely grained, and of much value to the state.

The peculiar growth of several groups in the Santa Cruz Grove, standing, as they do, in a circle, with their roots intermingling, seems to point to the probability that they, gigantic as they seem, are but younger children of some giant mother whose proportions would have dwarfed them to pigmies. This peculiarity of redwood growth is apparent everywhere in the forests of to-day; no sooner has one of the mighty ones fallen than there spring up around its roots a circle of tall, young shoots, representing all the features of the parent tree. Those who have explored the "Big Basin," a vast tract of totally unbroken virgin forest northeast of the mountain village of Boulder, say that other groves showing individual specimens quite as large as those here described are to be found there.

There are a number of other groves of Big Trees in California which we did not visit, but the Mariposa and Santa Cruz groups are as good types as can be found, and are worth a deal of trouble and pains to see. One can go to the latter grove with comfort; of the ride to the former and then out to the railroad, my impressions are still vivid and painful; but as it is "better to have loved and lost, than never to have loved at all," so may I say, it is better to have seen these wonders, though at such a cost, than never to have looked upon them.

## XXII

## HETCH-HETCHY VALLEY

AN INTERESTING LETTER — THE CAÑON OF THE TUOLUMNE — AN INDIAN HIDING PLACE — FISH AND GAME

WHILE publishing letters from California about the Yosemite Valley, I received a letter enclosing a most interesting account of a visit made by Rev. John D. Wells, D.D., of Brooklyn, and four companions, to the Hetch-Hetchy Valley, which has an appropriate place in this volume. This valley is an outlet of the cañon of the Tuolumne, a stream which runs for a part of its course parallel with the Merced River, and has many and beautiful waterfalls and grand, overhanging cliffs. Hetch-Hetchy is described as a smaller Yosemite, closely resembling the famous valley in its main features.

"*My Dear Dr. Stoddard:* I send you an account of a visit made by the Rev. Arthur Crosby, of San Rafael, his son and two other boys, and myself in the summer of 1887, to Hetch-Hetchy Valley, while we were on our way to Yosemite. It may possibly come in somewhere with your interesting letters from and about California and its wonders, many of which I saw.

"On the second day of May, 1887, I left home for the Pacific coast. In the fall of that year I gave four free lectures to my people, and others who cared to hear them. One was on 'The Valleys of California, especially Hetch-Hetchy and Yosemite.'

"I have read your letters with interest, following you from place to place, and greatly enjoying your incidents of travel, and your vivid descriptions of what, in many cases, I saw with my own eyes. But you did not travel in a conveyance at your own disposal, with good saddle-horses beside, for a whole month. So we travelled, — two men, and three nice boys about fifteen years old, and school companions. Moreover, we camped under the open heavens without rain or dew, visiting the valley whose name heads this article, Yosemite, and the Calaveras big tree groves, north and south.

"Not one in a thousand of excursionists to Yosemite turns out of his way to visit Hetch-Hetchy. The multitude go through by stage, and are impatient of delay. I am not sure that any party but ours — other than men in charge of sheep and horses, and some Indians — had entered it for years, and I learned after my lecture that some wide-awake sightseers, with time and money at their disposal, and quite at home in the Sierras, were incredulous as to the existence of the valley.

"We reached Crocker's, within twenty-two miles of Yosemite, on Saturday, intending to push on to the great valley that afternoon, but we yielded to the earnest request that we would spend the Sabbath there, and preach to people who seldom heard a sermon. It was while there that we heard of Hetch-Hetchy, and were strongly advised to visit it. Accordingly, Monday, June 13, we left at Crocker's all superfluous belongings, and turned from the main road abruptly to the north — with all our beasts — for a drive and a ride of about nineteen miles, to a veritable valley hid among the munitions of rocks, and reached only by the obscurest of roads and the hardest of trails. We lost our way more than once, but it led us a charming route through woods, and by lakes and natural meadows, to Ackerson's Ranch, and after that to Hog Ranch, — still Hog Ranch on the maps, though blooded sheep long since took the place of swine.

"Then we packed our beds and provisions on Pet and Prince, the saddle-horses, and bidding adieu for the time to our teamster, and to Gee, our Chinese cook, we two men and three boys, and jubilant Buck, the dog, struck into the hard trail for a tramp to the valley. We were in the higher, but not the highest, Sierras. However, they were high enough for our wind and muscle. It is one thing to climb eight or ten thousand feet toward the stars, with iron horses to puff and tug all the way up, while you sit at your ease on cushioned seats, and quite another thing to puff and tug for yourself. But there is no easier way to reach the interesting locality of which I write.

"Hetch-Hetchy Valley became known to white men in 1867. Long before, it was a hiding-place for Indians, and it is still visited from year to year by Pah Utes for the purpose of gathering acorns from majestic trees, under some of which we found shelter from the sun.

"In the summer of 1873, the remarkable cañon of the Tuolumne River east and a little north of Hetch-Hetchy was explored to Soda Springs, a distance of about twenty-two miles.

"We enter the valley on the southwest, after hours of toil, and feel at once the power of its mingled, yet contrasted, beauty and grandeur. There are, in fact, two valleys, the western — into which our trail brought us by a sharp descent — being a mile in length and from an eighth to the half of a mile in width. It was the pasture ground of about twenty mares and their colts, gleaming in the sunlight as if groomed by an hostler every day.

"The eastern valley is about two miles long and of ranging width, though nowhere more than half a mile. It was the pasture ground of sheep, and is parted from the western valley by a bold spur of granite from the south, reaching quite to the Tuolumne River. In this spur there is a depression through which a path leads from valley to valley.

"Out of these narrow cañons snow waters issue, making up the Tuolumne that waters the valley as a whole. Having done this service, and spread out its beauty to the sun, it passes into a narrow gorge at the west, — so narrow, indeed, that when the water is high in the spring it is dammed up, and the valley, from end to end, becomes a rock-bound lake. Then, too, a large body of water from the melting snows plunges over the lower rocks on the north, a thousand feet, into the lake below.

"I have yet to notice three of the most striking features of Hetch-Hetchy Valley. One is a perpendicular bluff on the north side, almost two thousand feet high, bearing a remarkable resemblance to El Capitan in Yosemite, which is thirty-two hundred feet high.

"Another is a waterfall bearing the name of the valley, and corresponding with Yosemite Fall. It is seventeen hundred feet from top to bottom, though not a sheer perpendicular drop.

"The third, and I think most impressive of all, is a triple dome on the south side, springing, not like the domes in Yosemite, from the stupendous walls of the valley, but a majestic object by itself, of vast diameter and height, forced up in plastic condition, with a second smaller dome surmounting it, and a third still smaller one surmounting the second. The third is fractured, but worthy the place it holds on the crown of a structure more majestic and enduring than the pyramids of Egypt, — the very 'weakness of God,' in nature as in grace, stronger than men.

"After this it may seem almost like sacrilege to add, that on the low pass between the two valleys, we saw the remnants of a sheep killed two nights before by a bear, and on a ride through the valley on Pet, far to the east, at the only cabin occupied by men, I saw the pelts of three sheep struck down at midday, only a few hours later, by the same or another bear.

"Moreover, the night we spent in the valley in the open air with a roaring fire at our feet, was made vocal, if not melodious and restful, by the unearthly yawling of wild-cats that could not agree to be neighborly, and were not willing to fight it out and have done with it. In the afternoon of the next day we repacked our blankets, and, repaid a thousand-fold for our visit, began our climb toward the crest of the rocks, up a winding and zigzag trail, and our tramp down to Hog Ranch. We spent Tuesday night at Hog Ranch, two of us sleeping in the house, and four, including the teamster, in the barn. And when we started for Crocker's, Wednesday morning, we were hardly out of sight of the house before we missed the road, so blind was the way, and went four miles before we knew certainly that we were wrong. Of course we were obliged to turn back and begin anew.

"On our way back to Crocker's, losing the trail, we saw four beautiful deer, and although we got no venison, we stocked our larder with two mountain pigeons, nearly twice the size of our Eastern birds, and a hundred and fifty trout from the middle fork of the Tuolumne River.

"The next day we entered Yosemite, that wonderful cathedral of God, down the graded road that brought us to the base of El Capitan, and just beneath the Royal Arches we camped two memorable days.

"Let me add that no one should go from Yosemite to Hetch-Hetchy, but reverse the order, as Hetch-Hetchy tones one's nerves for the awful depths and heights of Yosemite. We were thankful that we had seen the smaller valley and lower walls first.

"Yours sincerely,
"JOHN D. WELLS."

## XXIII

## EL MONTE

ROUGH TRAVELLING — MONTEREY — ITS FOUNDATION AND HISTORY — THE HOTEL DEL MONTE — AN ARTIFICIAL PARADISE — FLOWERS, SHRUBS, AND TREES — A PRIEST'S MONUMENT — THE OLD OAK — PACIFIC GROVE — THE SEVENTEEN-MILE DRIVE — SEALS, SHELLS, BUFFALOES, AND BEARS — STRANGE CYPRESSES

TRAVELLING in California is laborious, for the distances are long, the railroads winding, and their tracks unsettled, and the food stations far apart. The stage routes are over rough roads, where nothing but the sublime scenery and pure air would compensate for the jolting and jouncing to which the traveller is subjected. Many people travel, both for business and pleasure, and therefore trains, and coaches, and hotels are crowded. Under such conditions the traveller in California is fortunate to have some places of rest where he can not only "take his ease in his inn," but find all the comforts and luxuries which he requires. There are a number of such resorts in the state, notably at Coronado Beach, near San Diego, at Redondo Beach and Santa Monica, near Los Angeles, at Santa Barbara and Santa Cruz, and last and most famous of all, the Hotel del

Monte, near Monterey, on the Pacific, and a few hours' ride from San Francisco. There, after our long ride from Santa Barbara, having climbed the coast line of mountains, dined at Mojave, and swung around the fearful loop where the railroad doubles upon itself at a dizzy height, and breakfasted from our lunch-basket at Tracy, we came to anchor for a long and satisfying rest.

Monterey is one of the oldest towns of California, stretching along the bay of the same name, with adobe and brick and wooden houses, according to the date of their construction. Here, eighteen years before the Pilgrims landed at Plymouth, Don Sebastian Vizcaino landed with two priests and a body of soldiers, and took possession of the country for Philip III. of Spain. A cross was erected and an altar raised, and the first mass celebrated on this part of the coast. The place was named in honor of the viceroy of Mexico, who was Count of Monterey, and the projector of the expedition. Unlike the New England landing, this at Monterey did not grow into a settlement for more than a century and one-half. In 1770, Father Junipero Serra, the founder of the Franciscan missions on these shores, whose name is still held in reverence and whose statue adorns a hill at Monterey, established a misson here, which was afterwards removed to Carmelo Valley, five miles from the Bay of Monterey. The old stone church then erected still stands, and beneath its sanctuary repose the bones of the venerable Franciscan and three of his associates. In 1813 the Spanish missions in California numbered twenty-one, with annual revenues of two millions of dollars. Then came their struggle with the Mexican Independents, the downfall of Spanish authority in Mexico, and with it the overthrow of the Franciscans, in 1822, and, finally, the abolition of the missions and the confiscation of their property in 1845.

In 1842, Commodore Jones, of the United States Navy, seized Monterey and held it for a short time; then he apologized and withdrew. In 1846, General John C. Frémont was here with his expedition, and in this same year of the Mexican War, Commodore Sloat planted the stars and stripes on the old Presidio and was appointed the military governor of the territory. In 1850, California was admitted into the Union, the state government was established at San José, San Francisco began to rise in business and enterprise, and Monterey ceased to be more than a health and seaside resort for the northern part of the state. It has that character and reputation now. Its weather is not so warm either in summer or winter as in other parts of California farther south, but the temperature is more even than can be found elsewhere. The January average is fifty degrees Fahrenheit, the July average sixty-five. In a period of five years, 1887 to 1892, the temperature was only four times over ninety degrees, and seven times at the freezing point. It was a sagacious choice which the Southern Pacific Railroad Company made of a place to build a hotel which would refresh the traveller with its salubrious atmosphere, while it charmed him with its lovely surroundings. Probably no greater success has been achieved in combining comfort, elegance, economy, and beauty in a seaside hotel, than at the Hotel del Monte at Monterey. I say this, not to advertise a place which for a dozen years has been the delight of thousands of tourists from all over the world; whose vistas are familiar to all lovers of art; whose gardens have merited the encomiums of so great a botanist as Professor Asa C. Gray, and of which the homely words of the Princess Louise to the manager of the hotel express the opinion of every guest: "You have the most beautiful place, and the cleanest and the best-kept hotel that I have ever visited in my travels."

What, then, are the charms of El Monte, besides its moderate prices, its exquisite neatness, and its dainty and delicious table? Let me name a few of them for the benefit of those who have not seen or read of the place.

In 1880, the railroad company opened the hotel. It is an immense building, occupying three sides of a hollow square, so large that sunlight floods the quadrangle all day long. Every room looks out upon a beautiful garden, filled with the choicest of flowers and plants and shrubs, and kept in perfect order under the supervision of one of the most skilful and practical gardeners in the world. No foreign gardens that I have seen are finer or more varied, more delicate or lovely, than El Monte. Nature offers advantages of climate and soil which do not exist in any other civilized regions of the earth, and of these Mr. Clack, the gardener, has availed himself to the utmost. The building, with its spacious halls and large public rooms, where comfort and neatness are visible on every side, has wide verandas and inclosed piazzas, many staircases and conveniences on every floor, airy and light rooms, parlors, and music halls, and everything white and clean, warm and well ventilated, restful to eye and ear and brain. If I were a nervous invalid and craved repose in the midst of a garden of delights, I should come here and secure a room in one of the long wings, and sit at the window and listen to the distant murmur of the waves on the bay-shore, or to the song of the meadow larks on the lawns, and look out upon the flower-beds, where art and nature have worked together to produce most wonderful effects, or into the depths of the forest of liveoak and lofty pines, which were provided as the setting for this grand palace of delights, till my weary brain was flooded with quiet beauty, and life-giving and health-producing impressions began to drive out tiresome thoughts and wearying fancies. Many have done so, and yet this is not so much a resort for the sick and the invalid as a place of rest for the tired, a temporary home for tourists and travellers, and a resort for residents of the Northwest and of the Pacific coast. Some guests come from the East, and make the place their home during those months when Boston, and New York, and Philadelphia are wrapped in snow and vexed with wild winter winds.

"El Monte" means "the forest," and the Spanish name is the simplest and most truthful that could be given to the place, for while the hotel stands in a large and lovely garden, the garden is encircled by a forest of liveoak, pine, and cedar trees, of great size and incalculable age. Here the strange and distorted combinations of trunks and limbs which characterize the California liveoaks, are gracefully hidden or modified by sweeping draperies of moss, or deftly guided ivy and myrtle vines. Vast lawns of green myrtle, gemmed with large blue flowers, stretch beneath the trees; in the midst of a circle of tall trees an Arizona garden with every variety of cactus, from the smallest needle to the towering yucca, and the wide-spreading aloe, suddenly appears; a curious and formally trimmed cypress "maze" invites the vagrant pleasure-seeker to lose himself in its verdant toils; a lake, curving about beautifully wooded shores, offers boats safe and free to all guests to navigate its hidden bays and verdurous recesses; concealed from view by dense thickets, parties are playing tennis and croquet and bowls in open courts with ample sunshine and abundant room. About three hundred feet distant from the main building, in a grand grove and garden, stands the club-house, where gentlemen and ladies resort for bowling and other indoor sports; while down by the bay, a few hundred yards from the hotel, is the glass-roofed bathing pavilion, where salt and fresh water at any temperature are provided in great swimming tanks, over which hang baskets of blooming plants, and on whose decks stand tropical plants of all sorts. These are some of the pleasant features of this charming place, all of which may be enhanced by agreeable company and a happy disposition.

That I may not be charged with exaggeration, let me add the words of another writer upon the place.

He says: "In the midst of the forest sits the Hotel del Monte, with its one hundred and twenty-six acres of garden, — the finest, the most gorgeous, the richest, the most varied in all the world, the famous gardens of Kew and Kensington not excepted. It is not alone in summer that flowers bloom; in the middle of winter the grounds are lively with the color of blooming roses, pansies, and countless other flowers, while stretches of the tenderest plants, with callas and heliotropes in prominent lead, are seen on every hand. The marvellous ribbon beds, with minute details of infinite variety of forms and combinations, exist in all their beauty throughout the year, and the section called 'Arizona' — made up entirely of cacti, many of extreme sensitiveness to cold — remains continually in prickly and rebellious thrift. Ivy, honey-suckles, and nasturtiums grow in rampant luxuriousness, kept in decorous limits only by the free use of shears. In January and February, the first grand burst of spring color comes in the form of great beds of narcissus, tulips, crocuses, crown imperials, and the whole long list of Holland gems, arranged in beds of conventional design, in ribbons of dazzling colors, in trefoils, hearts, and every conceivable form. All the rare and beautiful flowering plants of countries south of the equator have found a congenial home in these grounds, and as their native summers are coincident with our winters, and as in their own countries they are summer-blooming plants, the habit in time of bloom which is a part of their nature, persists in transplantation; and this soft climate encourages this habit, so that during the winter months there may be seen in this vast flower-garden, plants that exist nowhere else in Europe or North America outside of some isolated or cramped conservatories." The local conditions for the culture of flowers are not equalled in the world, and there are great stretches of blue grass lawns between smooth and clean roads and walks where the daintiest shoe would not be soiled.

Every place has its pleasant and special features. El Monte is especially noted for the natural beauties which capital and labor in a happy union have produced and gathered there. But there are outside objects of interest which aid in making Monterey an attractive and desirable place for rest and recreation.

There are short drives along the beach to the famous old oak, whose gnarled and widespreading branches cover half an acre, and under which a Sunday school could sit; or to the statue of Father Junipero Serra, who landed at Monterey in 1770. This statue stands on a high bluff overlooking the bay, not far from the town, and was erected by the wife of the late Senator Stanford. Or one can take the street-car which runs through Monterey, goes on to Pacific Grove, and ends at Lake Majella among the sand-hills.

Pacific Grove was begun as a Methodist camp-meeting ground. The pine forest and the delicious sea air united to make the place attractive, and its proximity to San Francisco added to its popularity. It was laid out in lots, as Asbury Park and Oak Bluffs and other Eastern places were, at first, and tents and cloth shelters on wooden frames were set up. But as the place became known cottages were built, then shops, and soon the population increased beyond all expectation. Prices advanced, the Pacific Improvement Company was formed, and took in one section after another, till now the town covers an area of more than two square miles, has many handsome and expensive houses, good hotels, and beautiful flowers and flower-gardens. The place is noted for piety and prohibition. My driver said, emphatically: "There's one place in California where you can't get drunk." He seemed surprised when I told him that there were other places of the same character in the state. But though he had driven a great many miles for many years, he had not travelled far, and did not know as much as I did about California.

Pacific Grove is not a place for Sunday carousals and demoralizing sport. Its government is patriarchal, and it is a home for the pious, the cultured, and the gentle people who love to meet with the Women's Christian Temperance Union, the Chautauqua Assembly, the Sunday-school Convention, and similar assemblies. There are woodland sports and sea pleasures near at hand for all who seek the place, and I do not wonder that many persons come from windy San Francisco to the calm and restful pine forest which crowns this peninsula.

Just beyond the grove is a government lighthouse built of granite on Point Pinos. There the huge rollers of the western ocean swing their vast masses over the rocks, and dash upon the sand whole gardens of seaweed and clouds of spray. It is fascinating to sit on Moss Beach and watch this roaring, seething tide, and then to walk away into the dense woods where one may see a deer and sometimes a wild-cat, or to sit a little way from the sandy shore embowered in roses and geraniums and fragrant lilies.

The Pacific Improvement Company, one of the convenient names for the all-embracing Southern Pacific Railroad, owns a tract of seven thousand acres on this pine-clad point, and to bring the property into notice, as well as to entertain its patrons, it has constructed a beautiful drive which is called the seventeen, eighteen, or nineteen mile drive, according to the condition of the road, the horses, and the driver. I have taken it under different circumstances, and am quite sure that it varies in length, like the sea serpent. The route is through the town of Monterey, then into the heart of Pacific Grove, and on till near Moss Beach, which is left upon the right as we come out upon the shore of the Pacific. The views here are grand, and the ocean surf, when the wind is favorable, is as fine as I have seen on any coast. A short distance from the shore, a lofty and jagged island of rock rises from the water. It is covered with huge birds and seals. There are far more of these curious creatures here than at San Francisco, or at any point of the coast south of Alaska. As no shooting is permitted, the seals are tame, and it is a strange and interesting sight to watch their clumsy motions out of the water and their grace when in it. They fill the air with barks which sound like the voice of a dog with a cold in his head, and the gulls sing an appropriate soprano.

The driver of the four-in-hand has his curios to exhibit. He has pointed out a lonely Chinaman who lives on the rocks in a cabin made of rough boulders, and sells shells and fish, and now he calls attention to a marvellous gigantic ostrich, which is discovered to be formed of two distant cypress trees; then we are introduced to Buffalo Park, where can be seen that almost extinct animal, a grizzly bear, which delights to play with a jet of water from the hose of a fire engine, and beautiful collections of pressed seaweeds and polished shells.

The most interesting feature of the whole drive, however, is Cypress Point. Here, and in this neighborhood, there is a large number of the strangest trees that a traveller has ever seen. They bear some resemblance to the cedars of Lebanon, and also to those of Southern Italy, but they are more wind-twisted, gray, and weird than either of these. The bluffs are crowned with these strange growths, their roots and trunks clinging to and grasping rock and crag with fierce tenacity and desperate strength, their tops flat and spreading like an umbrella that shrinks before the gale and yet defies it. They are unique in their grotesque attitudes and grim resemblance to martyrs and tortured captives. They will not yield to their tormentors, nor bow down before them. So far as it is possible, they will fulfil the laws of their being, will grow towards heaven, and spread out branches and leaves into the sunlight; they will live and not die, and bear their fruit according to their kind. But the struggle, which has evidently been going on for centuries, is a terrible one, and they are wrenched and torn and distorted by winter storms that have dashed upon them in wild fury after a terrific race over four thousand miles of ocean, and they are grizzled and gray with centuries of mist and salt spray. Yet they stand here, moss-hung monsters, giving evidence, according to some judges, that they are not of Spanish origin, that they are not a growth from cedar of Lebanon seeds brought by pious missionaries, but rather that they were old when Christianity was young, and living long before Columbus sailed from Palos. How these things are discovered I do not know, but judging by their appearance, they are very venerable and afflicted trees, and I felt profoundly respectful and sorry for them, as I would for an aged Mohammedan undergoing the bastinado.

We passed on to the long and sandy Pescadero Beach looking out to Lobos Point, and then turning towards Monterey, came to the crest of the ridge which runs out from the mainland towards the waters of Carmel Bay. The views from this ridge in every direction are superb, and at a swift trot we swung down over a fine road into the town and the grounds of El Monte. We had been gone four hours, but we lingered by the way. We tried it again in a light wagon, and found that one can spin around the drive in two hours, and also that a whole day is none too long for a picnic.

This is but a sample excursion. One can find pleasant company here, and many walks and drives to pass the time. Among many agreeable leaves that I turn in the book of memory, a very pleasant one is inscribed, El Monte and Monterey.

CYPRESS GROUP, MONTEREY

## XXIV

## IN THE SANTA CLARA VALLEY

INCIDENTS AT SANTA CRUZ — SAN JOSÉ — CHURCHES, PUBLIC BUILDINGS, AND SCHOOLS — LICK OBSERVATORY — LELAND STANFORD JUNIOR UNIVERSITY — PALO ALTO STABLES — TRAINING SCHOOL FOR FAST TROTTERS

FROM Monterey we went to Santa Cruz. A beautiful beach, fine fishing, and flowers in profusion are at this place, and on account of its mild and balmy air and sheltered situation, it is a favorite resort in winter for persons of delicate lungs. Here, too, Mr. Sullivan keeps a capital hotel, and provides a rare assortment of horses to take visitors to the "Big Trees." My companion in travel has, for excellent reasons, a decided antipathy to a skittish horse, and also to a railroad-crossing on grade. Our drive from Santa Cruz to the grove was for these reasons not one of unmixed delight. Mr. Sullivan's pair was badly matched. One horse sneezed as if afflicted with the asthma, and his mate became unmanageable at every sneeze. The driver, with the imagination of the far West, invented a story to account for the peculiarities of his team, which cannot be reproduced here. Suffice it to say that, between the sneezing of the horse and the apprehension of destruction at railroad-crossings, which were frequent and dangerous, our drive through the grand scenery of the cañon was thrilling and disagreeable in the extreme. It is better to take the narrow gauge road to the "Big Trees," stop an hour or two, and then go on through the mountains to the Santa Clara Valley. This road runs through fine scenery, and comes out from wild mountain gorges into the beautiful and well cultivated region in which San José, one of the earliest and most substantial of California towns, is built.

The town is the country seat of Santa Clara County, and the chief city in the Santa Clara Valley. It is at the northern end of the valley, and only five miles distant from the southern arm of San Francisco Bay. It was founded in 1777 by the Spaniards, who had just established the Santa Clara Mission. There is a population of more than twenty thousand in the town, which is handsomely laid out with fine private residences standing in well-kept gardens, and costly and imposing public buildings. There is a State Normal School finely situated in a cultivated park of twenty-seven acres, a new city hall of noble proportions surrounded by a beautiful park, and the handsomest court-house in the State outside of San Francisco. The churches are numerous, and most of them have elegant and costly edifices. Besides a public-school system which is said to rival those of Eastern cities, there is the College of Notre Dame, located in an inclosure of ten acres within the city limits, and the University of the Pacific, under the direction of the Methodist Conference. Its numerous and elegant buildings occupy twelve acres, and include an astronomical observatory and a conservatory of music. On the site of the old Santa Clara Mission, three miles from San José, the Jesuits have a college, well equipped with libraries and philosophical and scientific apparatus. Its chapel is the old church erected by the Franciscan missionaries, and its garden, placed in an inclosed court, is full of rare and beautiful plants. A fine avenue, three miles in length, bordered by ancient trees, connects Santa Clara and San José. Electric lights and railways contribute to the comfort and convenience of the citizens.

At San José we spent several days, one of which was the Sabbath. Several of the pastors were absent, attending the convention of the Young People's Society of Christian Endeavor, which was held at Fresno. We found the pastor of the First Presbyterian Church, Rev. Dr. Densmore, lately of Denver, in his pulpit, and heard an eloquent sermon. Every seat was occupied, and the services were warm and hearty.

As I sat with the minister in his study in the afternoon, there was a knock at the door, and a young man came in. In a few words he told his errand. A law had just been put in operation which closed all the saloons in the city on Sunday. A similar law had already closed the places in the county outside, where liquor could be had. This Sunday closing had driven all the frequenters of the saloons into the streets. The parks were full of young men lounging on the seats, and there were crowds at every corner in the lower part of the town. The young man had come to the pastor for help to seize the opportunity to do these outsiders some good. "I have got a melodeon and a man to play," said he, "and now I want some young men to go with me and sing, and help conduct meetings in the parks. There is a great chance to catch some fish in the gospel net." The pastor thought so, too. He looked through his notebook. "Most of my young men are down at the convention at Fresno," said he; "but there is Bissell, who can sing and pray, and Walters, who is a fair speaker"; and he rapidly named a half a dozen others, giving their addresses, and a word or two of advice. "Perhaps you can lead some of them to our evening service," said he. With thanks for the help received, the young Christian went away, and there were a dozen extempore prayer-meetings that night, in the parks and streets of San José. This is the way things are done in the West. It is not necessary to have a religious debate in the session every time an opportunity occurs to save souls. The pastor is alive, the young people are alive. Christians have to be alive, for the devil is very much alive and still thinks that he has a pre-emptive right upon the men of the Pacific slope. But the Christian people are steadily gaining ground, and those who have lived since 1849 know what wonderful changes have been wrought.

One change, however, has not been for the better. I refer to the Chinese immigration and its results. Almost every city has a Chinese quarter, and it is usually the worst place in town, filthy, densely populated, full of opium joints, and a menace to physical and moral health. As I came from Dr. Densmore's study, a Chinese funeral was passing down the street. There were from twenty to thirty carriages full of people beating a gong and scattering pieces of paper along the highway to keep off the demons. Behind the carriages came a wagon containing baskets of food, and a live pig which was to be offered to an idol, or to placate the supposed evil spirits who were hostile to the departed.

It was a most repulsive spectacle of heathenism in a Christian land, the most public and unpleasant which had then met my eyes. Afterwards in San Francisco I saw Chinatown in its full extent, and also saw the faithful efforts which are being made in schools and churches to convert the Chinese to the Christian religion, and to deliver them from their bondage to opium.

The distance from San José to the James Lick Observatory on Mount Hamilton and return is fifty-six miles. The trip is usually made in one day, though some persons prefer to spend the night at Smith Creek, seven miles from the Observatory, where there is an indifferent hotel, and thus divide the journey. There is no accommodation for man and beast upon the summit unless they belong to the Observatory corps. An early start is needful, and good company is essential in so long a drive.

The first four miles gradually ascend to the foot-hills where the Observatory Road begins. This road was built on a uniform grade, over mountain and valley to the summit of Mount Hamilton. In selecting Mount Hamilton as the site for the Observatory, Mr. Lick made it a condition that the county of Santa Clara should build to the summit a better road than any in California. The condition was faithfully executed at a cost of seventy-eight thousand dollars, and its grade was so carefully planned that the rise is less than seven feet in the hundred. In order to secure this grade, it was necessary to wind along hill-sides and make sharp turns and long reaches, so that the distance traversed is nearly three times the direct line, and there are three hundred and sixty-five curves. But there are few places in the road where even a timid person would tremble, and the road-bed is as smooth and well-kept as any in the world.

Turning from the long avenue which leads to the foot-hills, we began to ascend to the first station where relays of horses await the coaches. At the Grand View House a beautiful panorama of the Santa Clara Valley is spread out. The Coast ranges of mountains form the background, San José lies spread out like a map, and between and beyond are the cultivated ranches of the valley, lovely stretches of woodland, orchards, vineyards, gardens, and little villages. Soon we turn into Hall's Valley. Here are shady nooks, and green slopes, and trickling streams, and pictures of rural loveliness in rare variety. We pass two riders who are gathering in a herd of cattle. They pay no attention to the road, but ride up and down hill-sides and through streams and woodlands to "round up" their horses or other stock. They have the Mexican saddle on powerful horses, the coiled lariat hangs on its horn, and with their broad sombreros, and pistols in belt, they are a good type of the Californian ranchman. At Smith Creek Hotel, situated in a charming little valley, there is a lunch for all who wish refreshment, and pure spring water. This is seven miles from the Observatory, but these seven miles are steeper, and require at least two hours. The views are magnificent and constantly changing, and embrace the rugged slopes of the Santa Cruz Mountains; the Bay of San Francisco, whitened with many a sail; and, in the far distance, the glistening Pacific. In the opposite direction the San Joaquin Valley spreads its vast expanse to the foot-hills, beyond which rise the snow-crowned summits of the Sierras. Nearly all the way the dome of the Observatory is in sight, and if the sun is shining, it glistens and flashes in the clear air, at the turns of the road, deceiving the traveller by its apparent nearness.

Mount Hamilton is twenty miles southeast of San José, and rises 4209 feet above the sea-level. Professor Whitney says that from this spot more of the earth's surface is visible than from any known point upon the globe; and the translucent air and freedom from atmospheric disturbance attest the assertion that there are twice as many nights favorable to observation as are known elsewhere.

James Lick was born in Pennsylvania, in 1796. He was an eccentric man, but his gifts to the state of California reached several millions of dollars, and were for wise and beneficent purposes. He executed a trust deed for the erection of the Observatory in

1874, died in 1876, and it was 1880 before work was begun. It took eight years to level the summit, make the three million bricks for the buildings, construct the telescope, build the dome, and equip the Observatory.

The buildings stand in a park of 2581 acres, and include a main building composed of two domes connected by a long hall, with study-rooms, instrument-rooms, clock-rooms, work-rooms, and a library. The dome for the great telescope is at the south, and rests on the top of a tower built into the solid rock. The telescope cost two hundred thousand dollars. Its tube is sixty feet long, and weighs four tons. It rests upon an iron column thirty-seven feet high, and is so perfectly adjusted that it can be turned to any point in the heavens with ease and precision. The body of James Lick is buried in a tomb beneath the instrument.

The smaller dome and other buildings contain the transit instrument and meridian circle, spectroscopic and seismic apparatus, clocks and chronographs and meteorological instruments, and suites of rooms for the observers and their households.

Saturday evening is the time when the public is permitted to look through the great tube, and there is a large and curious crowd on such occasions. Our visit was on a different day. There were with our party about a dozen other visitors. We were met at the door by the old janitor, who is certainly as eccentric as ever Mr. Lick was, and who has been twice sent to the insane asylum. Knowledge of astronomy, however, has not addled his brains. On entering the building, his remark made to the party in general was, "You go in there'n' wait." The party obeyed. As the wait was tedious, some left the reception-room and began to look through the halls. "What are ye straggling all round the building for?" roared the old man. "Go in, I tell ye, and wait." He was promptly obeyed. In due time, regulated by some occult chronograph, we were taken through the rooms by this rude guide. "That's Mr. Lick," pointing to his portrait; "that's the road, 365 turns, and cost seventy-five thousand dollars," pointing to some plans; "them's meteors, shootin' stars, ye know; won't be such another batch o' stars till ninety-six,"—this accompanied with a shove at a series of photographs. Then he led us to the staircase leading to the dome. When we were in, he said: "Now sit down in a row, and I'll tell you all about it, an' then you can ask questions." We sat down around the circle, and listened to a string of loose statements and large figures, interspersed with orders to "keep still till I'm through." Then an old lady timidly asked: "Was Mr. Lick a scientist; did he know how to use instruments like these?" "No," said the guide, "he didn't know anythin', not a bit more'n you do."

There were no other questions, the exhibition was closed, and we took our carriage for the twenty-four mile ride down the hill. But we had seen the biggest telescope in the world in its lofty observatory, and were satisfied. If we had not spent many nights long years ago in sweeping the heavens with a small, but useful instrument, and gazed through other tubes in different parts of the world, it might have been worth while to have waited in line on a Saturday night to look through the Lick telescope for two minutes, and then drive down the mountain at midnight. More than a hundred people do this every week during the season, and are satisfied. The remarks on the hotel circular about "courteous guides" at the Observatory were not borne out by our experience, which was amusing rather than instructive.

The staff of astronomers at Lick Observatory is not adequate to the place. It comprises Professor Holden, the superintendent, Astronomer and Secretary Colton, and Professors Barnard, Schaeberle, and Campbell, with a few assistants. These men have done, and are doing, excellent work, but are altogether overweighted. Professor Holden, besides the duties of general superintendence and those connected with the charge of forwarding the result of each individual's work, is librarian, scientific correspondent, and editorial supervisor of the publications of the Astronomical Society. The great telescope is used two nights by Professors Holden and Colton for photographic purposes; two nights it is employed for spectroscopic observations, and two nights it is used by Barnard and Schaeberle for miscellaneous work. The meridian circle is in charge of the latter, and the twelve-inch and six-and-one-half-inch telescopes in that of the former. Professor Campbell attends to the time service.

One of the latest enterprises of the Observatory was the trip of Professor J. M. Schaeberle to Chile, to observe the total eclipse of the sun, on April 16th of

LICK OBSERVATORY, MOUNT HAMILTON

the year 1893. The funds for the undertaking were supplied by Mrs. Hearst, of San Francisco. To make these observations, the Professor had to travel nearly twelve thousand miles; and through an unhealthy country, where the transportation of his instruments was difficult, and the chances of success were small. But all obstacles yielded to the patience, perseverance, and skill of the enthusiastic astronomer, and he succeeded in making no less than fifty negatives of the eclipse, eight of which were larger than had ever before been secured of any eclipse. Such is the enthusiasm of science.

The drive home from Mount Hamilton was shorter in time than the ascent, but fifty-six miles, even over a good road, is a long carriage-ride, and we were ready for rest and refreshment when we swung into the grounds of the Hotel Vendome at San José.

One of our most interesting days was spent at the Leland Stanford Junior University. It was one of the most perfect of California days in the month of May when we drove over the Palo Alto stock farm, a tract of seventy-three hundred acres which belongs to the University. The noble gateway and the main quadrangle, two dormitories, a mechanical department, and a number of houses for the professors have been thus far erected.

The plan of Mr. Richardson was modelled from the cloisters of the San Antonio Mission, and is not, so far as completed, effective or impressive. The main buildings form a low quadrangle, inclosing a court 586 feet long and 286 feet wide. They are built of a dull yellow sandstone, and covered with red tiled roofs. On the inner side, the buildings are connected by a fine colonnade, and the arrangement of rooms is admirably adapted for the uses of the University. Seen from a distance, the building now looks like a vast manufactory, but the completed scheme includes an outer two-storied quadrangle with cloisters on the outside, a memorial arch, and a chapel. The University was founded by Mr. and Mrs. Leland Stanford, in memory of their only son, who died in 1884. They endowed it with property worth from twenty to thirty millions of dollars. Three immense estates were conveyed to a Board of Trustees, the principal to remain intact and the revenues to be used for the establishment and maintenance of the University. These are the Palo Alto farm, already mentioned, which was the homestead of the Stanford family, and the largest horse-breeding farm in the world; Vina ranch in Tehama County, comprising fifty thousand acres, of which four thousand are planted with vines, making it the largest known vineyard; and Gridley ranch in Butte County, comprising twenty thousand acres of the best wheat land in California.

The idea of the University, in the words of its founders, "came directly and largely from our son and only child, Leland, and in the belief that had he been spared to advise as to the disposition of our estate, he would have desired the devotion of a large portion thereof to this purpose, we will that for all time to come the institution hereby founded shall bear his name, and shall be known as the Leland Stanford Junior University."

The object of the University, as stated in its charter, is "to qualify students for personal success and direct usefulness in life;" and its purposes, "to promote the public welfare by exercising an influence in behalf of humanity and civilization, teaching the blessings of liberty regulated by law, and inculcating love and reverence for the great principles of government as derived from the inalienable rights of man to life, liberty, and the pursuit of happiness."

The nature, object, and purpose of the University, as described in the deed of trust are, in brief: "A university, with such seminaries of learning as shall make it of the highest grade, where mechanical training shall be given, and where agriculture in all its branches, together with the studies and exercises directed to the cultivation and enlargement of the mind shall be taught. From the kindergarten to the highest schools there will be no important branch of art, science, or mechanics that will not be taught here, and to these advantages male and female students will be equally entitled." The school is nonsectarian; the articles of endowment direct only that the existence of an all-wise God, obedience to His laws, and the immortality of the soul, shall be taught.

The corner-stone of the first building was laid on May 14, 1887, and on October 1, 1891, the Leland Stanford Junior University was formally opened. Dr. David S. Jordan was called from the Indiana State University to be president. In his address on that occasion Senator Stanford said: —

"I speak for Mrs. Stanford, as well as for myself,

for she has been my active and sympathetic coadjutor and is cograntor with me in the endowment and establishment of this university. In its behalf her prayers have gone forth that it may be a benefactor to humanity and receive the blessing of the Heavenly Father. For Mrs. Stanford and myself this ceremony marks an epoch in our lives, for we see in part the realization of the hopes and efforts of years; for you, faculty and students, the work begins now, and it is to commemorate this commencement of your labors that we are here assembled."

There were present at the opening a staff of fifty instructors and six hundred students, about one-third of whom were women. In 1893 there were eighty-two instructors and seven hundred and sixty-four students, representing nearly every state in the Union and every civilized country.

Since our visit, Mr. Stanford has died, but the University will go on under the able management of President Jordan, and with the fostering care of Mrs. Stanford, whose chief interest in life centres here.

We had letters of introduction to the president, and he courteously conducted us through a number of the class-rooms, including the chapel, gave us all needful information, and then put us in the charge of a polite assistant, who spent the morning in showing us the manifold objects of interest in this new and flourishing institution.

I am bound to say that, great as was the interest of the party in the educational department of the University, its chapel and lecture-rooms, the art building and dormitories, a still greater interest was developed by both ladies and gentlemen when we drove to the Palo Alto stables and paddocks. There are eleven hundred trotting horses and five hundred running horses here. The famous "Electioneer," "Electricity," "Arion," and "Advertiser," were taken out of their rooms, and uncovered for our inspection. Each horse has a groom, and each groom is as careful of his animal as a faithful nurse could be of a child. The horses are kept in long rows of rooms, which are carefully padded and kept perfectly clean. A variety of blankets and clothes of different thickness, forming a complete wardrobe, hang on the walls. Every detail of food and exercise and temperature is carefully attended to, and nothing omitted which would tend to produce the most perfect conditions of health and growth.

From this view of some of the finest results of training, we were taken into the training school for trotting horses. Here we saw the method of teaching which produces these results. A fine-bred colt of six months was let into a ring by the groom. The ring is an oval inclosure, roofed and lighted from above, with a floor of soft earth. Its outer portion is railed off with a low, firm rail, forming the track where the horse is to trot. The trainer stands in the centre of the ring with a long whip, and such visitors as are allowed stand quietly with him. The colt is first taught to walk around the ring, then to move faster and faster, always on a trot. The instant he breaks from a trot he is stopped by the trainer's voice or whip, both of which are used constantly. The animal is not whipped, but the whip is his guide ; now it cracks behind to stimulate his speed, now in front to bid him turn, now in the ring centre to tell him to stop. The intelligence of this horse, not yet six months old, was wonderful, but when he went out, and one after another of the yearlings came in, the exhibition became one of the most interesting developments of animal culture that I ever witnessed. The horses seemed to know every word and motion of their trainer, and the precision of their motion, their beautiful carriage, and almost intellectual perception of their own development and education, made us ask involuntarily: "Can the professors of the University get as good work from their pupils as these trainers get from their colts?"

Afterwards we saw some of the famous racers spin around the course where they are exercised, and marked the care with which they were rubbed and washed and clothed when they came in from trotting.

When the Rev. Dr. Irenæus Prime was once attending a General Assembly in Kentucky, a good Presbyterian, who was also the owner of a stock farm, took him over to his place. Now Dr. Prime, like some other ministers, was fond of a good horse, and knew something of the different breeds of fine horses. As he discoursed of the descendants of "Lexington" and "Blackhawk" and "Eclipse" and of Morgan mares, the elder became enthusiastic, and clapping him on the shoulder, said: "Mr. Prime, a man that knows as much about horses as you do, can have any church he wants in Kentucky." It was a new qualification for the Presbyterian pastorate, but there was more in the compliment than a tribute to equine knowledge. The man who thus interested the Kentucky farmer on his own topic, had the versatility and friendliness and true human sympathy that made him always and everywhere at home, and in many places his name is still a household word.

From the horses we went to the mausoleum built for the resting place of the beloved son whose monument is the University. It is a beautiful little temple in a garden of plants and flowers. There Senator Stanford has been buried, and it will be also the ultimate resting place of the bereaved widow and mother.

From these gardens we drove through vineyards and orchards, and afterwards to Menlo Park, a favorite residence of wealthy San Franciscans. The evening found us, after our long journeyings in California, at the Palace Hotel in San Francisco.

## XXV

## SAN FRANCISCO

DANA'S PROPHECY — CALIFORNIA OPTIMISM — THE CHINESE PROBLEM — A CURIOUS AND COMPOSITE CITY — BEAUTIFUL SUBURBS — A VISIT TO CHINATOWN — THE THEATRE AND OPIUM DENS — CHINESE MEN, WOMEN, AND CHILDREN — SAUSALITO, ROSS VALLEY, AND SAN RAFAEL — A SUDDEN SQUALL — THE PRESBYTERIAN SEMINARY — FRIENDS AND FESTIVITIES — SACRAMENTO

MORE than fifty years ago, Mr. Richard H. Dana, Jr., the Harvard student who made that memorable voyage to the California coast in the brig *Pilgrim*, which resulted in "Two Years before the Mast," wrote thus about San Francisco and its harbor: —

"We sailed down this magnificent bay with a light wind, the tide, which was running out, carrying us at the rate of four or five knots. We passed directly under the high cliff on which the Presidio is built, and stood into the middle of the bay, from whence we could see small bays, making up into the interior, on every side, large and beautifully wooded islands, and the mouths of several small rivers. If California ever becomes a prosperous country, this bay will be the centre of its prosperity. The abundance of wood and water, the extreme fertility of its shores, the excellence of its climate, which is as near to being perfect as any in the world, and its facilities for navigation, affording the best anchoring grounds in the whole western coast of America, all fit it for a place of great importance; and, indeed, it has attracted much attention, for the settlement of 'Yerba Buena,' where we lay at anchor, made chiefly by Americans and English, and which bids fair to become the most important trading place on the coast, at this time began to supply traders, Russian ships, and whalers, with their stores of wheat and frijoles."

Mr. Dana's prediction has been more than fulfilled. The sand-hills where he gathered wood for the galley fire are covered with costly dwellings; the shores where he beached his skiff are lined with solid warehouses, and the harbor in which the *Pilgrim* and an old Russian vessel were the largest craft, is now filled with hundreds of full-rigged ships, ocean-steamers, and vessels of all the maritime nations of the earth who contribute of their wealth to increase the resources of one of the most enterprising and prosperous commercial cities in the world.

A writer for a prize offered by a Boston paper, thus eloquently discourses upon some elements in the greatness of this growing city. It has the true California ring: —

"San Francisco is queen of the Pacific by the divine right of natural supremacy. She is a city of invincible necessity. The gold in the rocks and in the rivers laid her foundation. The silver stream from the mines of Nevada fostered her youth. Then the rains turned their drops to grains of golden wheat for her prosperity. Later the sunshine painted its most brilliant hues on the fruit and imprisoned itself in the vine for her well doing, while the soil by mystic chemistry of air and light and water poured into her lap with surpassing abundance the products of every temperate and semi-tropical clime. Nearly all the good fairies presided at her birth, and only the one in charge of the climate was chary in gifts.

"The Golden Gate made the sand-hills of the bay the predestined site of a great city. A cleft in the rocks admits the boundless waters of the Pacific into a sheltered basin forty miles in length by six to fifteen in width. There is not another harbor of any size, excepting San Diego, on the entire coast line from Valparaiso to Alaska. Two rivers tap the great San Joaquin Valley and flow into the bay, bringing to the city's doors the wealth of the interior. The position of San Francisco enables her to take tribute from sea and land. She commands the trade of the Orient and the South Seas, of Alaska to the north, and Central America to the south, with all the lands between. Inland is the garden of the earth. She sits at the portal and takes toll of the commerce that enters seaward, and of the wine, the olive, the orange, the raisin, and other fresh and dried fruits; of the grain, of the wool, and the precious metals that come from the vast territory of which she is the commercial sovereign. She is the distributing and shipping point for a region more than twelve hundred miles in extent, north and south, east and west. As yet it is comparatively unoccupied. Who can predict the magnitude of San Francisco, when every fertile acre of this magnificent domain is a sea of grain and a forest of bloom?"

There are prophets who do not take this rose-colored view of the future of the city of the "Golden Gate." They say that the march of empire is towards Oregon and Washington, that no agricultural state can ever compete with states which have great mining and lumbering and manufacturing interests; that San Francisco has ceased to be the distributing centre for the trade of the Pacific coast, and will in consequence cease to prosper. Such pessimists argue that a city built on so many hills, with such a costly and disagreeable method of transit as the cable-car, must yield in comparison with cities of easier grades, where wheeled vehicles can be freely used. It may be needful for San Francisco to establish manufactories, and to level its hills, and rebuild upon a better plan, but if these changes become necessities in order that it may hold its place in a rivalry with other towns, they will be made.

The large Chinese population, which is a fragment of Asia, wedged in the heart of the city, is also viewed by many as a serious menace to the prosperity of San Francisco. A separate and isolated nationality is here maintained, which nevertheless draws its life and support from the American citizens. American manufacturers and tradesmen cannot compete with the Chinese, for the Chinese work twelve and eighteen hours a day, and live upon the most meagre fare. A large proportion of the Chinese use opium, and they herd together in worse dens than can be found in any of the degraded quarters of our cities. They are industrious, peaceful, and most useful as servants, porters, and in many subordinate positions. They quarrel and gamble, and foster gross immorality among themselves, but their intercourse with other people is mostly that of business. Missions among them have little effect upon the majority of the people, though those individuals among them who become Christians are pious, benevolent, and sincere. Presbyterian and Methodist and other missions have been useful in rescuing Chinese girls from infamy, in establishing some small Chinese churches on the Pacific coast, and in providing helpers and laborers for the fields in China. The self-denial and patience of those faithful and veteran missionaries who have labored among the Chinese deserve the highest praise, but the mass of the Chinese remains comparatively unaffected.

No one visits San Francisco as a tourist without seeing Chinatown. It is a curious thing to see a foreign city within an American city. But here is a town of twenty thousand Chinese inhabitants in the very centre of San Francisco. Whole blocks are occupied by these Asiatics, who live and move and have their being according to their own heathen, and to us disgusting, customs. They literally swarm in the precincts which they occupy. They crowd in rooms and cellars and coops along the alleys, and we saw a roost under a wooden awning where two Chinamen manage to sleep and live, a place hardly large enough for a small flock of pigeons. Every sort of business and trade is carried on in these confined and contracted quarters. Of course the shops which are designed to attract Americans and secure their custom are roomy, well-lighted, and tastefully arranged, but when we come to the Chinese stores for Chinese customers, we find narrowness, crowding, dirt, and everything that is offensive to our civilization. Scrolls of red paper covered with Chinese characters, gaudy lanterns, and outlandish signs cover the doors and windows of the shops; eating-houses that display hideous and disgusting viands, gambling dens and vile resorts are huddled together in dreadful confusion. In the evening all the Chinese male population seems to be divided between the barbers and their victims. The Chinese are shaved from crown to chin, including eyebrows and ears, and when shaved they go to the theatre or to the opium debauch. We went to both places. The theatre was crowded, and we were placed upon the stage near the performers, to whom our presence seemed of no sort of importance. One man beat a huge gong, which combined with wind instruments to deafen us. The actors talked in high, squeaky voices, with many gestures and attitudes. The theatre was packed with a crowd of Chinamen intent upon the play. Not a woman was to be seen, and the actors taking women's parts were all men. The plays go on evening after evening for weeks and months, and are made up of life dramas, including murders and combats and trials, and manifold episodes of Chinese life. Under the stage, and in the cellar of the building, are the rooms where the actors live, closely crowded together in ill-smelling and dirty quarters. With a guide who knew the labyrinthine mazes of Chinatown, we visited the opium dens, where wrecks of humanity lay on shelves of pine wood smoking the nauseous drug. Some of the men were lean and yellow skeletons, who seemed to have hardly strength enough to fill their little brass pipes with opium pills, and all the faces were repulsive and painful to look upon. We were taken to see one horrid old crone who was said to have occupied the same den for twenty years or more; she was blind and deformed and covered with rags, and in the midst of vermin and vileness. Mrs. Mackay, the wife of the many times millionaire, came after us, and left twenty dollars in gold for this wretched being, who is said to be a miser and have a miser's wealth stowed away in her miserable den.

After such dreadful scenes, it was a relief to go to the joss-house and see the idols to whom the Chinese burn incense, and in an elegant and spacious apartment to be served with delicious tea and a variety of candies and sweetmeats. In a back room some Chinese were gambling, and we watched the game for a few minutes. There were two women in this room and they were deeply interested in the game, laughing and clapping when the cards favored them, and showing abundant signs of displeasure when the luck went against them. The game was being played around a table where a feast had been in progress, and was evidently part of a festivity. Women are not often seen in the streets, but there are plenty of fat, short-legged, moon-faced children all over Chinatown. They are dressed in purple and yellow and green garments, their faces contrasting strangely with the wrinkled and drawn visages of their elders.

Chinese goods are very attractive to Eastern pilgrims, and we invested much money in crêpes and silks and thin porcelain and bronzes, and were not sorry to have done so when we came to give mementos of our journey to our dear five hundred friends at home.

To a visitor, San Francisco seems curious and composite. All races and tongues mingle here. Men and boys seem to be in a large majority, and the tone of public life and manners is roughened by the predominance of the male element. The great number of wooden dwellings, even the costliest and largest buildings being of this material, excites surprise. The numerous cable-cars, sliding and climbing in every direction with great rapidity and with incessant ringing of gongs, over the many hills of the city, give an air of noise and bustle to every part of the town. The climate is disagreeable. The mornings are usually pleasant, except in July and August, when fogs prevail, but each afternoon a high wind blows, whirling the sand and dust about the streets, and this wind is often accompanied with a chilly temperature which demands a fire in order to be comfortable. But in spite of this drawback to San Francisco as a residence, it is said to be one of the most healthy and highly valued homes upon the Pacific coast.

Some of our friends live in the suburb of Sausalito, across the water from San Francisco. It is a charming place, warmer than the city by several degrees, and sheltered from the winds and fogs which come driving in through the Golden Gate from the Pacific Ocean. We had a specimen of these winds on our excursion. All the vessels at anchor were blown from their moorings, the yachts were unable to ride out the sudden gale, and small boats had to make a speedy landing or be overturned in the bay. On the heights of Sausalito we watched the tempest, and were glad to be in safety and comfort with pleasant company during such a war of the elements. High winds are the bane of San Francisco, and in August come also disagreeable fogs, that make rheumatic people ache, and give the blues to timid and anxious souls. On the other side of San Francisco lies Berkeley, where the University and the Deaf and Dumb Institution are placed in the midst of charming scenery and a lavish wealth of flowers and verdure. It was a pleasant thing to see on each boat that came to the city from the suburbs, bunches of flowers in every hand, and often baskets of flowers which were being brought over as presents to city friends.

The Palace Hotel was our home while in San Francisco. It is a good enough hotel for any city in the world, and its rooms are comfortable and convenient beyond anything in this country outside of New York.

One afternoon we took the train for Sacramento, and in the morning saw there the State House, and all that was worth the traveller's time and patience. It is not an attractive place, even though it is the seat of government, and we were glad to bid it farewell and steam away into the fastness of the Sierra Nevada, upon the homeward track.

# XXVI

## ACROSS THE SIERRA TO SALT LAKE

SACRAMENTO TO CAPE HORN — SILVER MINING — AMONG THE SNOW-SHEDS — DESERTS AND INDIANS — GREAT SALT LAKE — THE SACRED INCLOSURE — TABERNACLE AND TEMPLE — THE LION HOUSE AND THE BEEHIVE — A THRIVING CITY — A RÉSUMÉ OF MORMON HISTORY — THE CREED AND GOVERNMENT OF THE CHURCH — FORT DOUGLAS

WE left Sacramento, with its costly Capitol, beautiful parks, and Crocker Art Gallery, about noon, and soon began to climb the Sierra Nevada. This name means "Snowy Range." The range lies west of the Rocky Mountains, and runs from Oregon, where it is called "Cascade Mountains," to the southern part of California. It is the western chain of the Cordilleras, and contains some of the highest peaks on the continent, such as Mounts Whitney, Shasta, and Corcoran, each of which is over fourteen thousand feet high. The peaks which inclose the Yosemite Valley are a part of this range, and its average elevation is from eight to ten thousand feet above sea-level. The scenery is in the highest degree picturesque, becoming grander as the road ascends. Cape Horn was reached early in the afternoon. It is a mountain promontory where the railroad doubles on itself, passing around on a little shelf two thousand feet above the American River, which winds its silver thread in the deep valley. Far off to the right is a ravine inclosed in mountain walls. In neighboring gulches and cañons, we saw many traces of mining operations; whole hills had been washed away by the powerful hydraulic jets which had been directed against them. Work was still going on in a few places, though the profit of silver mining was steadily declining.

With two, and sometimes three engines, our heavy train, now divided into two sections, climbed up the giant wall of the Sierra Nevada. We passed through the magnificent scenery of Shady Run, Blue Cañon, and Giant and Emigrant Gaps. In running one hundred and seven miles, we had climbed nearly seven thousand feet, sometimes over very steep grades. Before we reached the summit, snow-sheds began to appear, and soon became practically continuous. It was the month of May, and the mountains were still covered deep with snow. We rode through forty miles of these wooden tunnels, from whose windows we could now and then catch glances of wild wastes of snow-covered mountains, and at other times of forests of pine and fir trees. Without these sheds it would be impossible to operate the road in winter. They are built in the most thorough manner, often upon solid foundations of masonry, and are separated by iron plates into sections, to guard against the spread of fire. There are automatic electric fire alarms in one of the longest sheds, and an

ROUNDING CAPE HORN, SIERRA NEVADA

engine with a tank close at hand is kept ready to
flood any section that should catch fire. The sheds
are patrolled and guarded in a careful manner.
Such attention is due not only to the passenger and
freight traffic which the road conducts, but to the
value of the sheds, which averages from eight to
twelve thousand dollars per mile. Several miles,
where bridges and precipices made the construction
difficult, cost as much as thirty thousand dollars per
mile. The lover of picturesque scenery is grievously
disappointed as the train plunges into these utilita-
rian devices, but railroads are primarily for transportation, and scenery holds a second place with
civil engineers and boards of directors. If we had
been crossing the Sierra Nevada in a winter snow-
storm, I fancy there would have been no words of
complaint about the long snow-sheds.

From Summit, the railway slides down the eastern
slope of the mountains, following the course of the
rapid Truckee River, until it reaches the great inclosed continental plateau, an extensive level at a
height of four thousand feet above the sea. We
were now in the great and thinly settled state of
Nevada, a region of more than one hundred thousand
square miles, with a few moderate-sized towns and
many mining camps. It is the silver mining state,
and is full of bold and rugged mountains and wide
stretches of desert plain. The Southern Pacific
route from San Francisco to Ogden traverses four
hundred and fifty-six miles of this state, winding
among its snow-capped mountains and bringing the
benefits of civilization into its separated towns. At

some of the stations we saw Indians of the Shoshone and Piute tribes, and at one place an Indian squaw drove a brisk trade while the train waited, by exhibiting a pappoose to the ladies at ten cents a sight. All day we journeyed through an uninteresting and mostly desert country, a lonely and uninhabitable waste. I had never realized that so much of the United States was as truly a desert as the Sahara. It is said that only water is needed to make it all arable, but this is a desperate need, for only the snows of winter lodged in the far-off mountains can furnish irrigation to these deserts. We talked of the sufferings of the pioneers who crossed these wastes to settle the Pacific Slopes, and of later emigrants who came for gold and silver before the railways had made the transit swift and easy, and most of us were glad that we lived in these modern days. It is astonishing how luxury and ease destroy even the wholesome taste for romantic experience and adventure. The kid-gloved and perfumed aristocrat whose every want is provided for, in an "all around the world" trip, may have a "good time" in his sense of the word, but he misses many things that give variety and zest to travel and make its reminiscences a pleasure and delight.

Towards afternoon we came to Kelton, in the territory of Utah, and soon began to see the shores of the Great Salt Lake. This remarkable inland sea occupies about three thousand square miles, being ninety-three miles long and forty-three miles wide. It is at an elevation of more than four thousand feet above the ocean, is sixty feet deep, and has a number of small islands and two of considerable size. The water is very dense, being more than ten per cent heavier than the ocean, and only surpassed by the Dead Sea of Palestine in density. Bathers can float with ease in its waters, but they are acrid and bitter to the taste.

The sight of this expanse of water was an immense relief after the dreariness of the desert. The mountains surrounding the basin are picturesque in form and curious in coloring. Here and there are bathing places, but the shores are generally barren and uninhabited, except by station masters or employés of the railroad. We saw the Promontory Point, where the Union Pacific and Central Pacific Railways joined their iron bands, and where the last spike of the great railroad enterprise was driven, and then we sped away, with the noble Wahsatch range of mountains confronting us like a wall, towards Ogden, our point of detour in the visit to Salt Lake City, which is forty miles to the south.

Most of the way the mountains were on one side and the lake upon the other, and the scenery was fine. All the Mormon country in the springtime looked like the garden of the Lord, fruitful and flowery, and showed careful cultivation. Now and then a heavy cloud of smoke disfigured earth and sky, where a huge silver smelter voided its chemical fumes into the atmosphere, but in general the air was pure and the landscape inviting. Our train drew up at a neat and well-kept station, where well-horsed carriages were waiting in numbers to convey us through the city of Brigham Young and his followers.

From Ogden we came to Salt Lake City. It was a beautiful morning when we arrived at this town with so strange a history, and took carriages to ride through and about it. The city is situated four thousand three hundred feet above the level of the sea, in the same elevated valley containing the Great Salt Lake, which lies fifteen miles westward. It is protected by the lofty range of the Wahsatch and Oquirrh Mountains, which rise many thousands of feet above the town, at a distance of from fifteen to twenty miles. On leaving the train, we first drove to Prospect Hill, from which we could look down upon the place and see the wide and rectangular streets of the city shaded with trees. The business blocks, hotels, and churches stand in the lower part of the town, not far from Temple Block, which is the sacred square of the Mormons. This square contains ten acres, which are inclosed by a high adobe wall, and within the inclosure stand the huge mushroom-shaped Tabernacle, and the new Temple, which has just been dedicated. The Tabernacle has a roof like a turtle shell or a mushroom, supported by forty-four stone pillars. It is an immense, uninteresting building, capable of holding from eight to twelve thousand people. The former number could all be seated. Its acoustic properties are perfect. We heard a whisper and a pin drop across the vast space, and the performance for our benefit upon the organ was a remarkable exhibition of sound effects.

The temple is a large and handsome building of granite, with three lofty towers at each end. On the highest tower at the eastern end stands a colossal gilded angel. The interior is devoted to the secret rites of the church. There is a large sea or baptismal font, supported by bronze oxen as in Solomon's Temple, and many costly and beautiful offerings. Since the dedication — in 1893 — no Gentiles have been allowed to pollute this holy place, but the Tabernacle is used for many public purposes, and may be entered by any one. The Assembly Hall is a granite building in the southwestern part of the grounds, and is used for religious services. It contains wall paintings of scenes in Mormon history. The grounds in which these buildings stand are neatly kept and planted with trees and flowers.

This Zion of the "Latter Day Saints," as the Mormons prefer to be called, is a pleasant and thriving place. Besides the Mormon temples, there are churches belonging to the Gentiles, and among them a sightly and attractive Presbyterian church is prominent. The houses are mostly small, but very neat, and many of them stand in gardens or orchards. The Mormons are a thrifty people, and the farms and mines and manufactures of Utah show conclusively how prosperous the territory is, and how great a state Utah might become, if it were freed from the domination of the sect whose cruelties and abominations have disgraced the nineteenth century in this land. Among the show-places in Salt Lake City are the Lion House, one of the residences of the late Brigham Young, which has a carved lion over the entrance; another called the Beehive House, which bears the emblem of Utah — a beehive — on its front; the Tithing Storehouse, where the Mormons pay their tithes in kind; and Brigham Young's grave, surrounded by an iron railing.

In the year 1844, the Mormons were driven from Missouri and Illinois by an outraged public sentiment. Their prophet, Joseph Smith, and his brother Hiram were lynched in Carthage jail in the state of Illinois on June 27, 1844, and after many disasters and wanderings, the remnant, under the leadership of Brigham Young, made their long and perilous pilgrimage across the plains to Salt Lake City. Here in the desert they found their "promised land," and began to plough and plant, to irrigate and cultivate the soil. Industry and perseverance have made the Utah valleys productive and rich beyond all expectation, and the Mormons have shown how the great deserts of Western America can be made to blossom as the rose. Mormon practices, under the name of religion, have aroused against this people the hostility of the nation, and their high-handed violation of the laws of the country has brought them into frequent collision with the government of the United States; but a copious immigration largely induced by agents, and a concentrated form of government which is of the most absolute type, have contributed to their growth and prosperity. The territory of Utah was organized in 1850, and Brigham Young became the first governor. The territory would doubtless long since have been admitted as a state, were it not for the fear that the Mormons, if freed from the control of the United States, would legalize polygamy and revive the abominations which have only been repressed by the strong arm of the general government.

The Gentile element is growing more and more powerful each year, and as the territory lies in the direct path of travel, its wealth and advantages are becoming known. It is not unlikely that in a few more years Mormon influence will so decline in comparison with the other elements in the territory that Utah will be permitted to take a place in the sisterhood of states.

Though the history of this sect has often been published, a brief résumé from trustworthy sources may not be out of place. Mormonism dates from 1820, when Joseph Smith became interested in religious matters during a revival in the town of Manchester, New York, where he lived. He was a youth of fourteen years of age, very thoughtful and conscientious. He asked God to direct him to decide which of the sects was right, and in answer saw a vision and was told that all sects were wrong. In future visions he was appointed to the priesthood of the Son of God, and directed to restore the true church on earth, which should last forever. He was also directed where to find the inspired history of the aborigines of America, engraven in ancient characters on metal plates. He was inspired to translate this into English, and to publish it in 1830; from English it has been translated and published in many languages. This is the Book of Mormon. A year previous, John the Baptist had appeared to Joseph Smith and his companion, Oliver Cowdery, and ordained them to the Aaronic priesthood; and in the same year, Peter, James, and John appeared to them and ordained them to the apostleship of the Melchisedec, or higher priesthood. This is Joseph Smith's account of the origin of Mormonism. The Church of Latter Day Saints was organized with six members, April 6, 1830, at Fayette, New York, by Smith. Twelve apostles, seventies, high priests, elders, bishops, priests, teachers, and deacons have been since ordained to the number of thousands. They have sent out agents into many nations to proselyte, and have been especially successful in the British Isles and in Scandinavia. The baptized converts now number several hundred thousand. The Latter Day Saints profess belief in God the Father, his Son, Jesus Christ, his atonement for sin, in the Holy Ghost, in faith, repentance, baptism by immersion for the remission of sins, the laying on of hands to impart the power of the Holy Ghost, the resurrection of the dead, and the judgment. They recognize divine authority as necessary in the call and ordination to preach the Gospel and administer the ordinances of the church. They believe in the religious orders named above, also in the revelations contained in the Bible, the Book of Mormon, and other inspired books. They hold to the sacredness and eternity of marriages. They look for the building of Jerusalem and Zion, and the personal reign of Christ on earth as King of kings and Lord of lords.

Such is a brief summary of the rise and doctrines of this strange people. They are a sect gathered out of many nations, mostly from the ignorant and superstitious, and from races of strong and animal passions. They have been governed and controlled with great sagacity by leaders of acknowledged ability, who are always to be found for such service among the children of men. Their belief is a mixture of Judaism, Christianity, and animalism, and their worship sentimental and devotional. Their presiding officer in the church is now Wilford Woodruff, with George Q. Cannon, who has been the territorial delegate in Congress, and Joseph F. Smith as his counsellors.

We did not care to linger long in such a city. While it was yet early we drove beyond the city limits to Fort Douglas, situated on a fine plateau five hundred feet higher than the city. An electric railway makes it easy for the soldiers to come into town and for the residents to go out to the military parades, but the Mormons have no love for the United States troops, and the visitors at parade and guard mounting are chiefly strangers. There are more troops at Fort Douglas than at any other Western military post. Among the soldiers on parade was one company of Indians, which compared favorably with the other soldiers, and seemed to have a specially warlike appearance. By the reports of all who have to do with them, trained Indians make excellent soldiers. We loitered about the fort, listening to the music of an excellent band, and enjoying the extensive view from the parade ground, and then drove back to town and took the train for the Denver and Rio Grande scenic route.

## XXVII

## CROSSING THE ROCKY MOUNTAINS

WILD AND GRAND SCENERY — NEW AND WONDERFUL HOT SPRINGS — SIX HUNDRED MILES FOR TWENTY-FIVE CENTS — TWO MILES UP IN THE AIR — LEADVILLE, COLORADO — THE COLLEGIATE MOUNTAINS — CLIMBING MARSHALL PASS — RAILROADS AS HIGH AS MOUNT BLANC — ENGINES PLAY HIDE AND SEEK — THE ROYAL GORGE — AN ENGINEERING FEAT — THE PITTSBURGH OF THE WEST

OUR homeward journey from Salt Lake City was resumed over the Denver, Rio Grande, and Western Railway, and the stages of travel were so arranged that we went through the grandest scenery of the route by daylight. We followed up the Jordan Valley for about fifty miles, passing through a well cultivated region, and came to Provo, a Mormon town situated on Utah Lake, a fresh-water lake whose outlet is the Jordan River. From Provo the railroad climbs by Spanish Creek over Soldier Summit, one of the lower passes of the Wahsatch range. The pass is named from the burial of a soldier of the Confederate army here. We had risen more than thirty-two hundred feet in the ninety-five miles that we had traversed since leaving Salt Lake City, and

CASTLE GATE, ROCKY MOUNTAINS

were now about seventy-five hundred feet above sea-level. The views were wild and grand, but not extended, for we were travelling among high mountains. The descent was along the valley of Price River for seventy miles, and beyond the junction of Price and Green rivers the road followed the Green River for more than two hundred miles.

A striking feature of this part of the route is found in the Price River Cañon, where the gorge narrows to a space barely sufficient for the passage of the river, and two pinnacles of brilliant-colored sandstone, rising to the height of five hundred feet, form the entrance. So remarkable is the resemblance of this natural formation to towers of human construction, that the name "Castle Gate" seems most appropriate to the entrance to the deep and narrow valley. All day we were among the mountains, following the Green River. This is a majestic and navigable stream which joins the Grand River ninety miles below the town of Green River, and the junction of these two forms the Colorado River. On one side are the Roan Mountains, whose cliffs are variegated in curious veins and lines, and on the other side rise the San Rafael Mountains. Beyond Utah the Colorado Desert opens before us — dry, bare, and dismal. The fantastic shapes of the Little Book cliffs relieve the monotony of the way, but we were glad to arrive at Grand Junction, from whence, following the left side of Grand River through fantastic cañons, long tunnels, and pretty mountain vales, we came to a new and thriving watering-place called Glenwood Springs.

Glenwood Springs is one of the largest of the thermal springs of this section. The outflow of ten of the larger springs is about eight thousand gallons a minute, or twenty times as much as all the fifty-seven springs at the Hot Springs in Arkansas combined. A few years ago the place was a part of an Indian reservation, and little was known of the springs which have since made the region so famous. The town is simply accessory to the springs. These are situated at the junction of the Grand River and Roaring Fork, in a picturesque valley, fifty-two hundred feet above sea-level, surrounded by high hills which are still covered with native forests.

A fine hotel, which can accommodate several hundred guests, stands upon a terrace above the springs. Below the hotel is the bath-house, which with its pools and fountains cost several hundred thousand dollars. The "Big Pool" is probably the largest swimming pool of hot spring water in the world. It covers more than an acre, and the waters are freshly supplied from the hot springs, which pour into the great enclosure two thousand gallons per minute. From the midst of this great swimming-pool a fountain of cold water rises with graceful jets. The depth of the pool is gradual, from three and one-half to five and one-half feet; the walls are of red sandstone and the floor of smooth brick. The pool is without a roof, and beyond the broad stone coping there is a gravelled promenade. It is the custom of the place for people to walk around the pool and watch the bathers, and crowds may be seen in and out of the water on any fine morning. Within the elegant bath-house there are many private rooms fitted with porcelain tubs, besides parlors and reading-rooms and lounging-rooms. A physician also has an office here, and is in attendance all day. In addition to the tubs there are large private Roman baths of porcelain and glass, supplied with hot and cold showers, vapor cave baths, and every facility for Russian and Turkish treatment.

While we were at Glenwood Springs, two rival roads were running excursion trains from Denver, which is about three hundred miles distant. One road carried passengers for a dollar; the rival sold its tickets for twenty-five cents. Many inhabitants of Denver thought that it was cheaper to travel than to stay at home, and consequently the little town around Glenwood Springs was crowded to repletion. People who could not find beds slept on tables or settees, and we saw wearied couples who had sat up all night on chairs, thankful for shelter. As a natural result of such crowded excursion trains, the regular time-tables could not be maintained; there were some minor accidents, and the risk of many more. The hotels ran out of food and drink, and the prices of things to eat advanced in proportion to their scarcity. We were glad to have command of a well-stocked Pullman train upon which we had enough to eat and drink, and comfortable places to sleep. But our time-table was interfered with by these excursions, and also by several heavy landslides, which are not unusual in the cañons through which the Denver and Rio Grande Railroad winds its way.

We left Glenwood Springs about noon, and travelled through the cañon of the Grand River for eighteen or twenty miles. Its rocky sides rise in columns and battlements from two thousand to twenty-five hundred feet in height, and the full flowing river plunges and roars through this abyss. The darkness of the chasm, into which sunlight rarely falls, adds to the sublimity of the scene. There seems to be scanty room for the railway and the river, and one wonders at the hardihood which built a railroad in such a place. After this sublime experience, it was a relief to traverse an open and rolling country for thirty miles before repeating our emotions at Eagle River Cañon. For thirty miles or more the road climbs steadily, rising four thousand feet in that distance, and reaching, at the Tennessee Pass, a height of 10,440 feet above the sea. The scenery of the first part of the route is most majestic and interesting. We had come into the midst of one of the largest mining camps in the world. All along the almost perpendicular walls of the cañon, miners' dwellings were seen clinging to the rocks; the débris of the shafts, stagings, waterwheels, and mining paraphernalia met our view at every turn; the rocky heights, some of which were of a deep red color, broken into curious forms of gigantic birds and animals, or arranged in grand architectural designs of Egyptian proportions; the mountain peaks beyond that reared their dark forms far up into the heavens; the frequent waterfalls and the vast mass of the yellow torrent whirling through the gorge, joined to make the scene grand and impressive. The cañon ended almost abruptly at the picturesque mining town of Red Cliff, and we emerged into a more open, though very elevated country. Lofty mountains densely wooded on their slopes, sometimes bare and rough as they ended in domes and peaks far above us, were seen on every side, and among them the noble mountain of the Holy Cross. The engineering of the road is magnificent — it plunges through rocky spurs or winds around them; it doubles on itself and lifts its track to seemingly inaccessible heights, whence the traveller looks down with awe and wonder.

Passing by the Frémont Pass on a lower level, we came to the Tennessee Pass, and here crossed the Continental watershed at a height of nearly two miles above the sea. After steaming a dozen miles, we drew up at Leadville. Here all got out of the train and began to walk about, but some of the party at once felt dizzy, and many noticed an increased action of the heart, due to the rarity of the air. This town is finely situated at a height of ten thousand two hundred feet, among lofty mountains, and has a population of ten thousand, most of whom are interested in mining. It is an old town for this region, having been founded in 1859, under the name of California Gulch, and it was for many years one of the richest gold-washing camps in Colorado. It is said that during the first five years of its existence five millions of dollars' worth of gold dust was washed from the earth of this gulch. Then the place was nearly abandoned for ten years, till in 1876, extensive beds of carbonate silver were discovered, and a population reckoned as high as thirty thousand rushed in. The name of "Leadville" was given to the former "Gulch," and the annual yield of silver from the Leadville mines has been, till recently, about thirteen millions of dollars. We made a brief stop at this "city above the clouds," as it is sometimes called, and then commenced our rapid descent through the valley of the Arkansas River, between mighty hills, to Salida, where we stopped for the night to rest and prepare for an excursion on the next day to the famous Marshall Pass. These days among the Rocky Mountains give a traveller some conception of the wonders and novelties of this vast mountain range. We have only begun to explore its mysteries, to gather its wealth, and to study its manifold and sublime features. The future has much to reveal to the student and explorer in these rocky fastnesses which Wendell Phillips eloquently called the "ramparts of freedom."

Salida is a small town beautifully situated on the Arkansas River, commanding a grand mountain view. From a small hill in front of the station, the three "Collegiate" peaks of the Sawatch range, Mounts Yale, Princeton, and Harvard, each more than fourteen thousand feet in height and crowned with perpetual snow, fill the western horizon. In the south rise the snowy summits of the Sangre de Cristo range, and Mounts Ouray and Shavano in the southwest.

A special train was in waiting after breakfast to make an excursion to the Marshall Pass. The road went directly for the mountains, and soon was winding its way along steep embankments and shelving precipices. As the train drew near to the Poncho Pass, Mounts Shavano and Ouray, peaks named in honor of chiefs of the Ute tribe of Indians, became most prominent. The narrow gauge road leads towards Ouray. The mountain is fourteen thousand feet high, and the summit of the pass is 10,852 feet high. The road twists and turns, and doubles upon itself, so that at some points three and even four parts of the line seem parallel, until it comes out directly at the base of the great snow dome of the Ouray Mountain. The scenery on this road is of the grandest sort. Long ranges of snow-covered mountains, in cones and pyramids, all of which are within a few hundred feet of the height of Mount Blanc in Switzerland, greet the eye. Lower down, wooded heights fringe the snow line, and elevated valleys diversify the landscape. The prospect is not dreary and desolate, but sublime and inspiring, and the pass somewhat resembles the Stelvio Pass in Italian Switzerland, where the roadway reaches a height of ten thousand feet, and looks at once into the regions of perpetual snow and the cultivated valleys of the Tyrol.

The inevitable snow-sheds appeared as we ascended, and the actual top of the Marshall Pass, the continental divide upon which so much eloquence has been expended, is in the middle of a dingy construction of this sort. Here we were, sitting comfortably on the very ridgepole of the continent. I seemed to hear with new force those sermons and moral addresses which my youthful memory recalled, and of which the Marshall Pass was the star illustration.

The drop of water on the summit of this pass may be turned by the wind, by a tiny stone, by the slightest influence or obstacle to one side or the other of the ridge. How vast the difference of experience and result which hangs upon that alternative! Flowing to the east, it will join the rivers which fructify the fertile and far-extending continent, will water cultivated and peaceful regions, will contribute to inland navigation, to the development of valuable industries, the prosperity of a nation, the blessing of the world. Flowing to the west, after a wild and turbulent plunge over precipices, through gloomy cañons, lashed into foam, dizzied in whirlpools, torn by jagged rocks, out of sight in subterranean passages, or tortured by desert heat and hurried through uninhabited and inhospitable tracts of earth, it will bury a miserable existence in the lonely Pacific. Such and so important are the turning-points, the crises, in human lives, in national existence, in the history of an enterprise or of an institution. The simile is an admirable one, and it has been made to do frequent duty ever since the Marshall Pass was discovered. Doubtless it was used by orators and essayists long before, but the Rocky Mountains gave it a new prominence. And here we were, in such a classic spot, under a sooty shed, and the poetic drops were aggregating dirty pools along a cindery railway track. We climbed out of the train and found a door and a plank walk which led through the snow to a wind-swept frame tower. The blood mounted to the brain and the ears buzzed as with a dose of quinine while I climbed the staircase which lifted me to nearly eleven thousand feet above the sea-level. The wind came rushing through the pass like a cavalry squadron, bearing flurries of feathery snow; and the sun shone out, and far and wide the mountain landscape glittered and glowed in its beams. One does not care to stay long upon summits. They are briefly inspiring, but the work of the world is done lower down and mostly on the dull levels. Peter wanted three tabernacles on Mount Tabor, but the Master paid no attention to his remark, and the inspired narrator tells us that Peter wist not what he said.

We came down more rapidly than we went up, but with great care on the part of our engineer. He used gravity as a motive power and steam for the brakes. Our extra engine went ahead. It was a pretty play of "hide and seek" around the curves, and sometimes four terraces of the same track were below us, the lower one directly in front, six miles distant, and a thousand feet below. The maximum grade of the railway is two hundred and eleven feet to the mile, and there are curves that reach twenty-four degrees in one hundred feet. From Salida to Sargeant is forty-two miles, and one-half of the distance is taken up in crossing the Marshall Pass by zigzags. We were at Salida in time for dinner, and in the afternoon took one of the most picturesque journeys which has been embraced in our tour, down the Arkansas River. Five miles from Salida are the Wellsville Hot Springs, which are celebrated for their medicinal qualities; thence the road meanders down through broad valleys, following the Arkansas

River. Gradually the mountains close upon the river, which begins to rage and boil at its confinement, and reaches the climax of its fury as it flings itself into the jaws of the Royal Gorge. This is one of the most wonderful scenes in the transcontinental route. The rocks tower to a perpendicular height of twenty-six hundred feet, and through this defile the heaped-up waters of the Arkansas River rush and roar. It must have seemed madness to engineer a railroad through such a pass, but the men who planned the road have carried it out. The track is carried on a bridge which is literally hung from the smooth walls of rock on one side and braced by iron beams from the opposite precipice. The only equal engineering feat that I recall is where the Dalsland Canal at Hoverud, in Sweden, is carried across a river at a perilous height in an immense iron trough. The sensation during the transit of the Royal Gorge reminded me of my feelings years ago, when at the canal crossing on the Dalsland. This, however, has more elements of sublimity. The gorge is narrower, the precipices are much more lofty and perpendicular, and the river is larger and more awful in its fury.

Continuing down the Arkansas Cañon, we came to Cañon City, where miners and stockmen have their headquarters, where the climate is said to be perfect, and the mineral waters excellent, and soon after reached Pueblo. Pueblo is an active and handsomely built city, containing about twenty-five thousand inhabitants. It is called the "Pittsburgh of the West," and is the metropolis of south central

Colorado, and a great railway junction. Rolling-mills and iron works, and large smelters for the reduction of gold, silver, lead, and copper have been established here, and it has also a large business in agricultural products. There is nothing to detain the traveller unless he is interested in metal and mining industries, and after a short visit we resumed our journey. From Pueblo to Colorado Springs is one long panorama of magnificent scenery. Through the whole distance majestic mountains, broad plains sweeping eastward, and flourishing towns meet the eye. The mountains of which Pike's Peak is the prominent summit are always in sight. It was the evening of a day full of wonderful enjoyment among the great and awful works of the Creator, which found us in the full civilization and rest of one of the most famous health resorts of the nation, — Colorado Springs.

## XXVIII

## COLORADO SPRINGS, MANITOU, AND DENVER

THE INVALIDS' HOME — THE MINERAL SPRINGS OF MANITOU — "GARDEN OF THE GODS" — HELEN HUNT JACKSON'S GRAVE — PIKE'S PEAK — ITS DIFFICULTIES, WONDERS, AND GLORIES — THE CENTRAL CITY OF THE UNION — MINES AND INDUSTRIES — ENTERPRISING PEOPLE — DANIEL WEBSTER NO PROPHET — THE VIEW FROM CITY PARK — HOSPITALITY AND HOME FEELING — ON TO THE EXPOSITION — HOME AGAIN

COLORADO SPRINGS is a town of ten or twelve thousand inhabitants, handsomely laid out upon an elevated plateau, about six miles from the base of Pike's Peak. It has wide streets shaded with trees, trolley railways running in various directions, a great many handsome houses and fine churches, and a population largely composed of people of delicate lungs, who have found here a place where they can live with comfort. The town was founded in 1871, and it has been carefully preserved from the inroads of manufactures. Colorado College is located here, and the philanthropist, the late Mr. George W. Childs, of Philadelphia, here founded a home for decayed printers. There are educational institutions, and the state asylum for the deaf and dumb

PIKE'S PEAK FROM COLORADO SPRINGS

also here. No liquor saloons are allowed in the place, and the Sabbath that we spent at Colorado Springs had a New England character which was quite refreshing after the experiences of many of our Sundays. Rev. Livingston L. Taylor is the pastor of the First Presbyterian Church, a man of health and power, and with his church is alive to every hospitable and Christian duty, as well as earnest in the proclamation of the Gospel.

There are no "springs" nearer to the town than Manitou, about six miles away, where we passed some pleasant days, but Colorado Springs is nevertheless the right place for invalids to live in. Its climate is like that of the Engadine, but the mountains are not so near, while to the east and south of the town spreads a boundless table-land which continually recalls the ocean on a calm, mild day. The air is dry, the sunshine almost constant, and there is no frost nor melting snow, nor any rain from September to April. The town is sheltered by the foothills, except where the plateau extends on the southeast, and enjoys the openness and fresh air from the mountains; the soil is dry sand and gravel with a layer of loam on top; all water is brought from the mountains, and the sewerage and sanitary arrangements are excellent. There are many good physicians, excellent society, opportunities for riding, driving, and out-of-door amusement, and all the facilities for comfortable and happy life. The climate is said to be especially suited to consumptives or those who have a tendency to that disease. It is also recommended for debility and nervous exhaustion, but not adapted to the aged or to those who have organic nervous or heart troubles.

Six miles from Colorado Springs, situated in a small valley among the spurs of Pike's Peak, and at the mouth of Ute Pass, is Manitou Springs. There is not an acre of level ground in the valley, and the hotels and dwellings are perched on terraces and hillsides. Through an opening in the hills the snow-white crest of Pike's Peak is seen, and a cog-wheel railway makes the ascent an easy matter for the traveller. The springs are twelve in number, divided into three groups, and are situated on the banks of Fountain Creek, a stream that flows swiftly through the centre of the village, or on Ruxton's Creek, which comes from the Ute Pass. They have distinctive names, — Navajo, Shoshone, Manitou, Little Chief, and Iron. The water is impregnated with carbonate of soda, and is used for drinking and bathing. All day long people may be seen drinking and filling demijohns and bottles at the public fountains, and sometimes family wagons stop, and while the father fills the jug, the mother fills the numerous children with the healthful liquid.

Between the towns of Colorado Springs and Manitou, lies the far-famed "Garden of the Gods." Photographs and descriptions have made this place familiar, but none of them convey the grotesque and curious scene in its completeness to the mind. The "garden" is a tract of about five hundred acres in extent, inclosed by cliffs and hills, and thickly strewn with immense masses of red and white sandstone in most odd and fantastic shapes. The imagination runs riot in a place like this, and different groups of the sandstone have been named for animals and edifices and mythological monsters. A drive through the garden affords any number of fine views of the mountains and the table-lands, as well as an acquaintance with the geological wonders of the place; and it is usually taken in connection with a visit to Glen Eyrie, where General Palmer has produced a little paradise in the midst of the most fantastic scenery. The neighborhood is full of places of natural and personal interest. In one cañon a beautiful red sandstone is quarried, in another there are extensive silver mines, and high up on the mountain-side of South Cañon is the spot chosen by Helen Hunt Jackson for her burial-place. This celebrated author loved the South Cañon with its musical Seven Falls, and often resorted to it for recreation and musing, and in accordance with a desire frequently expressed in life, that this should be her last resting-place, she was buried here. It is a sad and gloomy place for a lonely grave, marked only by a pile of rocks which have been placed by literary admirers and sympathizing visitors upon the sacred spot. A drive up the Ute Pass, past Rainbow Falls on Fountain Creek, brings the visitor to the Grand Caverns, which contain fine formations of stalactites and stalagmites and flowering alabaster. There are also numerous fossils and bones of animals and men. There are a number of chambers and halls extending for nearly a mile underground, in some of which the lime formation is still going on, and in all of which the petrifactions are interesting and beautiful.

The great excursion from Manitou is to Pike's Peak. This is one of the best known summits of the Rocky Mountains. There is a carriage road which ascends by a comparatively easy grade in seventeen miles, a bridle-path, and a foot trail, all of which are used, but the majority who now make the ascent do so by the cog-wheel railway, which is about nine miles long, with a total rise of seventy-five hundred feet, an average of about eight hundred and fifty feet to the mile. It takes two hours to reach the top, and costs five dollars for the round trip. Major Zebulon Pike, whose name the mountain bears, tried nearly a century ago — in 1806 — to scale this lofty height. He succeeded in reaching the top of the neighboring mountain now called Cheyenne, but the difficulties beyond seemed so great that the attempt was abandoned, and he wrote that "no human being could ascend to that summit." It was fifty years before the ascent was known to be attempted again, and then a regular trail was made, and now and then a venturesome traveller scaled the mountain by this long and dangerous route. After 1870, new paths were made, and as the region had been much explored by miners and engineers, the ascent began to be more frequently attempted. In 1889 the first carriage road was built up the north and west sides of the mountain by frequent zigzags. By these ways travellers could make the trip in one, two, or three days, according to weather and strength. The idea of an iron railroad was published in 1884, but it was not realized until 1890. In October of that year a golden spike fastened the last rail in the highest railroad in the world, and made it easy to go in half a day to the top of this mountain, 14,147 feet above the sea. The road begins in Engleman's Cañon, near the Iron Springs, and climbs through wild and beautiful scenes, among forests, and ravines, and waterfalls, to the Half-way House. Thence over a level stretch, amid groves of pine and aspen, for more than two miles, from which point superb distant views are obtained; the road then goes on to a steep incline, at what is called Timber Line, 11,625 feet above the sea. A sharp turn is then made to climb into the "Saddle," and a steep rise of about eight hundred feet brings the train to the old government signal station, on the top of the peak.

Like most mountains, this veteran is coy and uncertain; snow-squalls and mists sometimes disappoint the tourist; but the climate of the region is so fine, the atmosphere so pure and dry, and the ascent so easily made, that with a fair day at command, one does not often descend unrewarded for his toil. The view from the summit is of vast extent, embracing the Buffalo Plains of Colorado, which stretch out north, south, and eastward in a seemingly endless level, like an ocean floor. Westward the eye roams over hundreds of snow-mantled mountains, whose peaks soar into the blue vault of heaven with every variety of outline. If the one view is of a calm, waveless ocean, the other view is of the same boundless ocean tossed by furious winds into huge masses of black and white billows which leap against the sky. Far below is the busy world and its clamor. Only the firmament above is unmoved in its blue and beautiful serenity. Looking into that clear space, it seems as if we can realize the presence of Him who sitteth on high above the floods of earth, who holds fast the mountains, or at whose touch they tremble and smoke; who has filled these mountains with gold and gems, and clothed them with majesty and power; who has spread abroad through Nature the evidence of His greatness, and among men the proofs of His goodness, and who will one day fill the whole earth with His glory.

Denver is the central city of the United States. It is a striking example of growth and prosperity. Situated in the midst of an arid country fifteen miles from the eastern base of the Rocky Mountains, a mile above the level of the sea, with no navigable rivers or lakes, it has yet developed, from one family living in a log cabin in 1857, into a city of one hundred and fifty thousand inhabitants, which contains many large, handsome, and substantial buildings, tasteful private residences and gardens, important industries and valuable manufactures. Sunshine, clear and stimulating air, the grand scenery of the Rocky Mountains, and a soil that responded to irrigation are at the foundation of the success of Denver. Next to these natural advantages, is its position in the heart of a rich mining district. Nearly all the known minerals exist in Colorado in happy distribution. Every valley where water is brought to develop the richness of the soil, is bounded by hills that contain either coal, iron, lead, copper, tin, zinc, gold, silver, lime, and building-stone; or deposits of salt, borax, oil, asphaltum, and textile clays. This position made the town a railway centre, a depot for supplies, and by natural growth, a city. Denver is not a rough Western city. It has an air of business and bustle, but not the reckless helter-skelter drive of Chicago. It more resembles Cleveland or Buffalo than the "Windy City," and the citizen of New York does not feel far from home among its people or in its streets. The population of Denver was gathered from the best of the settlers from the East. They were young men of courage, good judgment, and persistent energy, and they were also men of good character. The town was aggressive and yet conservative. Side by side with enterprising business and vast industries rose attractive homes, and commodious schools, well-equipped churches, and a university which has grown out of Colorado Seminary, founded in 1870, the same year in which the first locomotive entered the city.

The unrivalled growth of the United States has far outstripped the conceptions of our greatest statesmen. The speech of Webster in 1838, delivered in Congress upon the question of establishing a post-route from Independence, Missouri, to the mouth of the Columbia River, is one of the most striking illustrations of this statement. Daniel Webster opposed the bill, and closed his speech as follows: "What do we want with this vast, worthless area? this region of savages and wild beasts, of deserts, shifting sands, and whirlwinds of dust, of cactus and prairie-dogs? To what use could we ever hope to put these great deserts, or those endless mountain ranges, impregnable, and covered to their very base with eternal snow? What can we ever hope to do with the western coast, a coast of three thousand miles, rockbound, cheerless, uninviting, and not a harbor on it? What use have we for such a country? Mr. President, I will never vote one cent from the public treasury to place the Pacific coast one inch nearer to Boston than it now is." It was a two months' journey in those years from Boston to where Denver stands; we go now with ease and comfort in five days. In the midst of the "shifting sands" of this "worthless area" is the city of one hundred and fifty thousand inhabitants which American enterprise has built, not as a solitary Tadmor to show the power of a tyrant, but in response to the demand of a great people who have poured the waves of population into and over the desert, and made it a garden of wealth and beauty. We drove out through long and well-kept avenues lined with hundreds of small but well-built and neatly kept houses, to the City Park of three hundred and twenty acres. This public place is but partially laid out, but it gives promise of being a credit and a blessing to the city. From its roads one can see on the west the unbroken line of the Rocky Mountains, extending for nearly two hundred miles from Pike's Peak on the south to Long's Peak on the north, the summits crowned with snow. The city, with its new state capital and fine residences around it, forms a grand panorama on the east as seen from the park.

From the park we went to some of the smelting works, and watched the processes with interest from the time when the crude, crushed ore was dumped into wheelbarrows from the trains till, having passed through a variety of changes, it came out in large ingots of precious metal. The value of the ores reduced here in a single year (1891) amounted to twenty-four and one-half millions. A friend who has made the mining regions of Colorado his home for a dozen years, who knows all the mines and their products, and who, as a practical engineer, is familiar with these mineral industries, became our guide and instructor in Denver. He made me at home at the club, took me to see the assay of precious metals and the many places of interest in the town, and, with some other equally hospitable friends, aided in the formation of pleasant impressions upon my mind; but had I known no one in Denver, I should soon have made friends and found myself at home.

Here our tour of the South and West practically ended. We were two days in reaching Chicago, but the route was familiar, and our faces and thoughts were turned towards the great Columbian Exhibition, then in the fulness of its glory. It has now passed like the others which preceded it, among which it was the largest and most wonderful. Its beauties and peculiarities have been pictured and described again and again, till all the reading world knows them by heart. After a couple of weeks at Chicago, on a summer day we arrived once more in New York, with hearts full of gratitude for safety and health through months of travel, and memories stored with pictures, which, better than any photographs, reproduce for us the varied and instructive scenes of this long journey in some of the grandest and most beautiful parts of our broad land. He who has drunk of the fountain of Trevi in Rome is sure to return to the Eternal City, and so one who has breathed the pure and delicious air of the Pacific coast, and wintered in Pasadena, Santa Barbara, or El Monte, longs to shake off the wintry snow from his feet and seek once more the orange orchards, the rose gardens, and the balmy breezes of the Golden State, or the dry and exhilarating atmosphere of the Rocky Mountains. I have long since said good-by to those travelling companions with whom so many delightful days were spent, and now as a guide, I say adieu to the great company of readers and friends whom I have personally conducted through the Southern and Western regions of our great country.

Norwood Press:
J. S. Cushing & Co. — Berwick & Smith.
Boston, Mass., U.S.A.

**DR. STODDARD'S OTHER BOOKS OF TRAVEL.**

# ACROSS RUSSIA

## FROM THE BALTIC TO THE DANUBE.

*ILLUSTRATED.* 12mo. $1.50.

---

### PRESS NOTICES.

"Dr. Stoddard has all the primary essentials of a tourist, eyes to see, ears to hear, with a well-pronounced faculty of keeping the precious metal separate from the dross. . . . He made good use of his time and of his opportunities, and we but do him justice when we say that we know of no book on the same subject in which so much useful, readable, enjoyable matter is to be found." — *Christian at Work.*

"A most interesting volume. . . . A keen eye, a ready wit, and great felicity of expression have enabled the author to present to the public a book of travels quite out of the ordinary style. While truthful as sober history, it is as charming as a novel." — *New York Journal of Commerce.*

"The volume has many fine illustrations. Mr. Stoddard is a good traveller; he sees well, and his descriptions of people and places are graphic and of large value. . . . Our author takes in all the leading cities, sees what there is to see of art, visits and describes the famous palaces and churches and hospitals, and makes his book as profitable as it is pleasing." — *Chicago Inter-Ocean.*

"In the easy style of a traveller, he tells his readers what is worth telling, and leaves the rest unsaid. . . . The great works of art, the imposing churches, the capacious palaces, all are described in a concise yet satisfactory manner, as well as the customs, religious and otherwise, of the people." — *Christian Intelligencer.*

"The author of this book sets before his readers vivid pictures of this interesting country and people." — *United Presbyterian, Pittsburgh.*

"Mr. Stoddard seems to have had exceptional opportunities to study objects of interest, and writes about them in a way that cannot fail to interest. We have had so many dark pictures of Russia lately that it is a pleasure to get hold of a book that is to a certain degree optimistic. The book is well illustrated." — *The School Journal.*

"The eyes through which we look in this pleasant volume of travels are not unused to sight seeing, and the descriptions here given are entertaining and happy." — *Herald and Presbyter, Cincinnati.*

"The volume richly deserves a place among those welcome helps that are bringing the most distant and unfrequented parts of the earth near to our own doors." — *Golden Rule, Boston.*

# SPANISH CITIES

## WITH GLIMPSES OF GIBRALTAR AND TANGIER.

*ILLUSTRATED.* **12mo. $1.50.**

### PRESS NOTICES.

"He fulfils the ideal of a delightful travelling companion, whose conversation has informing qualities without being tedious, and whose style has sparkle and flavor without froth." — *New York Tribune.*

"His style is direct, easy, and graceful, and his strong English sentences have need of few adjectives to enforce their meaning. His descriptions of places are concise and yet clear, and so markedly elegant as to deserve more than usual commendation." — *Chicago Inter-Ocean.*

"Dr. Stoddard's style is easy and flowing, and he gives us, not merely a chronicle of where he went and what he saw, but he gives us a series of delightful pen pictures of Spain and its people, their habits and customs and modes of life. There are several excellent illustrations which add much to the interest of the work." — *Boston Daily Advertiser.*

"An unusually fresh and beautiful book of travel." — *Brooklyn Daily Eagle.*

"A straightforward, unpretentious, interesting account of travel in Spain, with interesting descriptions of cities, and passing notes of Spanish life without tiresome statistics or historical rehashing." — *The Independent.*

"A writer who has the power of seeing things as well as describing what he sees. To read it is to take one of the most delightful trips conceivable with a charming companion and raconteur. . . . The illustrations are from photographs, and add very much to the attractiveness of the volume." — *The Detroit Free Press.*

"He knows well how to find the points and the persons of special interest, and then understands how to make what interests himself seem vivid and of similar interest to the reader. His style, while pure and simple, is picturesque and easily appeals to the reader's imagination." — *The Advance.*

"Dr. Stoddard is a traveller who knows what he wants to see, and sees it, and a writer who knows how to make his readers see what he has seen. In this pleasant tour in Spain he saw the present and recalled the past, and his sketches of what he saw gain an added touch of romance from the glimpses he gives of what he remembered of their former history." — *The Evangelist.*

**CHARLES SCRIBNER'S SONS, Publishers,**
743 and 745 BROADWAY, NEW YORK CITY.

www.ingramcontent.com/pod-product-compliance
Lightning Source LLC
Chambersburg PA
CBHW031942230426
43672CB00010B/2022